Bottom One Pan Sausage Supper (page 40); *centre*, Savoury Mince with Crumble Thatch (page 37); *top*, Clapping Eggs (page 37).

DEAN

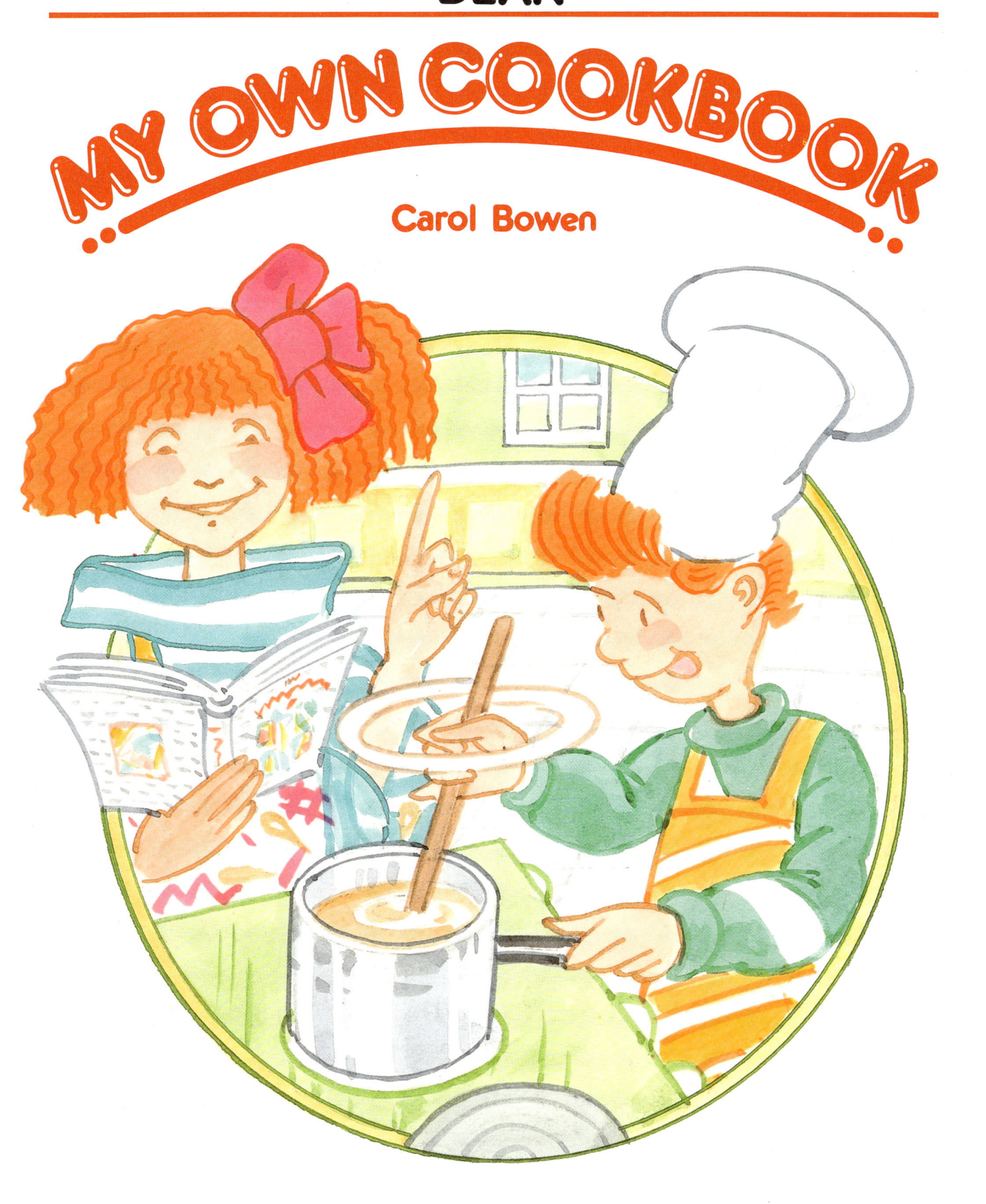

MY OWN COOKBOOK

Carol Bowen

For Lucy

The Publisher would like to thank in particular
the following for their help and co-operation
in providing accessories for photography:

British Home Stores, London

Strangeways, London
for watches, clocks and sunglasses

Illustrations by Robin Lawrie

Photography by Chris Crofton

Home Economist Lyn Rutherford

Photographic Styling Andrea Lambton

Back cover The back cover illustration shows,
bottom left, Speedy Pizza (page 40);
top centre, Hot Air Balloon Cake (page 49);
bottom right, Cheddar Sails (page 44).

First published in 1985 by
Deans International Publishing
52–54 Southwark Street, London SE1 1UA
A division of The Hamlyn Publishing Group Limited
London · New York · Sydney · Toronto

Copyright © Deans International Publishing a division of
The Hamlyn Publishing Group Limited 1985

ISBN 0 603 00704 X

All rights reserved. No part of this publication may be reproduced,
stored in a retrieval system, or transmitted, in any form or by any means,
electronic, mechanical, photocopying, recording or otherwise,
without the permission of
Deans International Publishing.

Printed and bound by Purnell and Sons (Book Production) Ltd.,
Paulton, Bristol.
Member of BPCC plc

CONTENTS

Introduction 7

Safety in the Kitchen: the Cook's Code 8

Basic Kitchen Tools and Techniques 9

Recipes to Get You Started! 12

Better Breakfasts 18

Sizzling Snacks 24

Fantastic Family Fare 34

Special Occasion Cookery 44

Outdoor Food and Food for Free 50

Foodie Gifts to Make 56

Index 61

INTRODUCTION

Cooking is great fun and any dish, simple or special, prepared and cooked for friends or family, brings great satisfaction.

Cooking isn't difficult, although if this is your first attempt you can be forgiven for thinking it is. It is simply a matter of learning and mastering, then never forgetting to check, the basics of food preparation.

Once learnt, the basics can then be given your own treatment – this is where the fun really begins – and when reputations are made!

Concentrate at first on perfecting the basics like making a light-as-air sponge or crisp and flaky pastry, then proceed to developing new flavours, shapes and fillings that you think will look and taste good.

The boundaries, as you will happily discover, are limitless and can be explored over the years. It is my delight to welcome you to the world of cooking! Have fun.

Carol Bowen

SAFETY IN THE KITCHEN

✓ always concentrate on the job you are doing and do not try to do two things at once

✓ always wear an apron

✓ always wash your hands before you begin

✓ always read the recipe all the way through before you start to cook

✓ make sure you have all the utensils you need before you start to cook

✓ collect and weigh out all the ingredients you need before you begin and put them away afterwards

✓ always use a pair of oven gloves to handle hot shelves, dishes or saucepan handles and when using the grill

✓ always turn saucepan handles towards the back of the cooker away from you – take care that no handles are over other heated rings or elements

✓ wash up as you go along keeping the kitchen clean and tidy – it is never much fun washing up a pile of dishes at the end

✓ if you're not sure about anything in a recipe then do ask a grown-up

✓ if you're small, get a grown-up to switch on the oven or grill

✓ follow the recipe step by step – don't be tempted to take shortcuts

✓ keep calm

✗ never fool about in the kitchen especially with sharp knives or hot food – never rush about

✗ never touch any electrical sockets with wet hands

✗ never plug in appliances that are already switched on – switch off first

The Oven – Your Most Important Tool

Any visit to a gas, electric or solid fuel showroom will demonstrate just how many different types of cookers there are on the market. Each with a vast array of special features ranging from ceramic hobs, spark ignition, fan assistance, automatic timing, automatic cleaning etc.

Your oven handbook will give a guidance to making the best of these special features but fundamentally all ovens (with the exception of microwave) are the same – that is to say, they cook using the principles of temperature over time. The oven temperatures used in the recipes in this book can be used for all three types of ovens – gas, electric and solid fuel in both °C and °F. The table on the right gives their recommended equivalents:

	°C	°F	Gas Mark
Very cool	110	225	$\frac{1}{4}$
	120	250	$\frac{1}{2}$
Cool	140	275	1
	150	300	2
Moderate	160	325	3
	180	350	4
Moderately hot	190	375	5
	200	400	6
Hot	220	425	7
	230	450	8
Very hot	240	475	9

BASIC KITCHEN TOOLS AND TECHNIQUES

There is no doubt that a few good kitchen tools can speed up and ease the tricky or boring aspects of some parts of food preparation. It is wise to make sure the kitchen is provided with the few basics. Specialist items can be added as and when they seem worthwhile.

Knives
If you have a good selection of knives in your basic tool kit then you are bound to find the ideal one for the task in hand. As a minimum have a large knife (for cutting meat and bread), a medium knife (for cutting pastry) and a small knife (for paring and chopping vegetables). Treat them with care. They're to cut food not your fingers.

A palette knife is useful for spreading pastry fillings evenly and one with a serrated edge is excellent for cutting and serving flans and quiches. A fish slice will also prove useful.

Scissors
Almost any task that a knife will perform scissors will also do. Use for trimming, cutting and to snip herbs such as chives.

Cooling Rack
A wire cooling rack is essential for cooling cakes and crisping small and large pastries. Choose a large all-purpose one for maximum use.

Weighing Scales
Scales are an absolute must to make sure that ingredients are in the correct proportions. Always follow one set of measures, Imperial or metric, since the quantities are not interchangeable.

Measuring Spoons
Measuring spoons are just as important as scales in measuring ingredients. Get a set that has a good range of sizes. Imperial spoons usually include $\frac{1}{4}$, $\frac{1}{2}$ and 1 teaspoon measures with a 1 tablespoon measure. A metric set will include 2.5, 5, 10 and 15 ml spoons. While on the subject of spoons, have a good selection of wooden spoons.

Measuring Jugs
A good selection will prove a worthwhile investment. Choose a variety of sizes from 300 ml/ $\frac{1}{2}$ pint, 600 ml/1 pint and 1 litre/$1\frac{3}{4}$ pint for eye level accuracy.

Rolling Pin
Choose a rolling pin that is long, even and without ridges for good overall use. Cool pins are also available especially for rolling out pastry – these are usually made of china, marble or glass and some are hollow to hold iced water. Lightly flour rolling pins before rolling out pastry and clean after use with a damp cloth.

Your rolling pin will find a multitude of other uses too – it will help in lifting pastry over pies and flans, in shaping pastry type biscuits before and after cooking, in crushing biscuits to make crumbs for cheesecake bases, and in giving a good clean cut edge to flans and tartlet moulds.

Pastry Brushes
A good selection of pastry brushes of varying sizes will prove invaluable for glazing pastries and tarts prior to baking. Smaller brushes are ideal for delicate decorative pieces and a larger one for large surface coating.

Piping Bags and Nozzles
Piping bags and nozzles will be needed for piping cream or cake icing. A selection of sizes and shapes will prove a good investment. Choose nylon piping bags that are easy to clean.

Sieves
A sieve will prove very useful in quickly and efficiently sifting flour with any other seasonings, flavourings or raising agents. A plastic sieve will often prove the easiest to clean. A sturdier metal type sieve will prove useful in puréeing some fruit fillings and sieving glazes prior to use.

Baking Trays
A large variety will prove useful in coping with all sorts of baking from large pastries to small party nibbles. A large flat tray is a good investment alongside a few with raised edges in case juices might leak out. When you can, choose the best quality since it will have endless uses from holding pizzas, shortbread, jalousies, pastry shapes and biscuits and will also act as a base for flan rings and bottomless frames. A baking tray is also useful when cooking pastries in ceramic dishes – a ceramic dish should be placed on a metal tray so that the heat is conducted more evenly to the base of the dish.

Flour Dredgers
A flour dredger is a must for sprinkling flour evenly over both work surface and rolling pin. It is also the foolproof way of making sure that you do not add too much flour with a heavy hand. There is a vast array available including metal, pottery, glass and china. Don't just use it for flour, it will prove useful for sprinkling sugar and spices over pies and tarts.

Pastry and Biscuit Cutters
Whatever the shape there is almost always a cutter available for it. Round fluted and plain pastry cutters are probably the only ones you will really need

frequently but you can choose from cocktail cutters, alphabet cutters, heart-shaped cutters, fruit-shaped cutters, fish-shaped cutters, aspic cutters, vol-au-vent cutters both round and square, etc.

Cling Film, Polythene and Foil
These are all useful in covering, wrapping and baking procedures. Wrap pastry while chilling in polythene, cling film or foil. Bake pastries 'blind' using greaseproof paper or foil and beans. Freeze foods in a freezer type polythene or foil for good storage and cover bread doughs with cling film during the rising and proving processes.

Chopping Boards
Choose a good thick chopping board made of a strong hardwood for cutting or chopping meat, vegetables, cheese and other items.

It is often the case that if you give any two people the same ingredients and recipe they will probably produce two different results. It may be a question of inaccurate measuring of ingredients but more than likely one of different handling.

To ensure that your results are good ones it is important to weigh accurately and to follow the techniques and procedures outlined in the methods faithfully. Some of the most common techniques used in the book are explained clearly below, read them now for background information and refer to them occasionally if in doubt.

Measuring Ingredients
This really is the most important technique I know, for if you get this technique wrong almost anything you do later cannot rectify the situation.

Measure all dry ingredients on a reliable set of scales or with special measuring spoons. Liquid measures should be measured in the same spoons or in a measuring jug – at eye level.

Only use one set of measures, Imperial or metric, since they are not interchangeable.

All the spoon measures given in the recipes are level ones unless otherwise stated.

Rubbing In Ingredients
This is a technique used in pastry, scone, some cake, biscuit and bread mixtures. Rub in with your fingertips, never be tempted to use the hot palms of your hands. Lift the mixture high and rub with the fingertips and thumbs to blend, allow to fall back into the bowl then lift again to continue. Rub in until the mixture resembles fine breadcrumbs or until the fat and flour are evenly mixed.

Creaming Ingredients
Creaming is a procedure principally used in cake making. It is a softening and blending process done to mix ingredients together until light and fluffy. Always use a wooden spoon to cream two ingredients together.

Saucepans
Good quality saucepans are essential since you are sure to use one size or another almost every time you cook. Those with thick heavy bases ensure that the heat spreads evenly for cooking. To ease on washing up you might like to use a saucepan with a non-stick surface.

Whisks, Beaters and Blenders
For general use, a simple flat whisk, as opposed to rotary, is probably the best. Clean thoroughly, in between the coiled structure, after using.

An electric whisk or blender is invaluable. Use according to the manufacturer's instructions. Remember always to turn off the electricity before pulling out or putting in the plug *then* switch on. *Never* immerse the machine body in water.

Folding Ingredients
Another blending process but quite different from creaming. Here ingredients are mixed together so that no volume is lost. It is essential to use a metal spoon that cuts through the mixture to lift, fold and mix.

It is a procedure most commonly used when mixing beaten egg whites or whipped cream into other ingredients.

Whipping Ingredients
A procedure used with cream to thicken and increase the volume.

Whisking Ingredients
This is a technique of beating ingredients with a whisk to introduce air. Foods like egg whites are whisked, for example to make light as air meringues. After whisking, a food is always folded with another to mix, never creamed or stirred.

Kneading Ingredients
Kneading can mean many things to different dishes. In the case of bread-making it implies a strong, sturdy pulling and stretching action to strengthen the bread dough prior to baking. To knead bread dough, form the dough into a ball then push down with the heel of your hand and push away from you with the palm. Give the dough a quarter turn, fold the dough towards you and repeat. Kneading usually takes 5 minutes or longer for any bread dough.

To knead pastry and biscuit doughs, simply press and turn the dough over gently a few times to form into a smooth ball free from cracks. This usually only takes about 1–2 minutes.

Puréeing Ingredients
This is a procedure used to make a smooth mixture either by beating, sieving or passing the food through an electric blender or food processor. If the food contains an acid, like fruit, then purée mixtures through a nylon rather than a metal sieve.

A selection of basic kitchen equipment.

RECIPES TO GET YOU STARTED!

Every cook has to start somewhere in learning the techniques of food preparation and cooking – there is no such thing as a born cook, just one who has cleverly practised and mastered the art of mixing, matching and serving foods at their best.

If you're a real beginner then you could do no better than to start at the very beginning and learn how to make a good cup of tea or coffee – reputations are often built on such humble beginnings! Progress to making other basic foods like an omelette, a boiled egg or a basic sandwich cake and you'll have all the expertise you need, literally at your fingertips, to cook the more complicated recipes that follow in the book.

How to Make a Good Cup of Coffee

The simplest way is to use instant coffee powder or granules. Place 1 teaspoon into a cup and add about 150 ml/¼ pint boiling water, water and milk or all milk. Stir well to blend.

Much more stylish and certainly more flavoursome is a cup of coffee made with ground coffee beans. Allow 1 tablespoon ground coffee (fine or medium ground) per person with 150 ml/¼ pint water. Unless you have a percolator or filter coffee machine the easiest way to prepare is by the jug method:

Warm a jug by adding a little boiling water then drain. Add the coffee and right amount of boiling water, cover the jug with a lid or a folded tea towel and leave to stand for 3–4 minutes. This is called 'infusing' the coffee. Strain through a sieve into cups or another warmed jug to serve with milk or cream if liked.

How to Make a Good Cup of Tea

Allow 1 teaspoon tea leaves or 1 tea bag per person and one for the pot when making tea for up to three people. For four people then still use only 4 teaspoons or 4 tea bags.

Warm the teapot by adding a little boiling water then drain. Add the tea leaves or tea bags. Bring the kettle to the boil but do not allow to continue boiling and pour immediately over the tea. Cover and leave to stand, or infuse, for 4–5 minutes. Strain, if necessary, into cups to serve.

Serve Indian tea with cold milk at breakfast and tea time and China tea mainly as a tea time drink with thin slices of lemon.

Basic Cooking of Eggs

Boiled Eggs

Eggs may be soft-boiled, with a softly set white and a runny yolk; medium-boiled, with a firm white and a just soft yolk; or hard-boiled with a firm white and dry, solid yolk.

Soft-boiled Eggs Bring a pan of cold water to boiling point over gentle heat and, with a spoon, carefully lower each egg into the water. Cook for the following times:

Grade 1 eggs	4½ minutes
Grade 2 and 3 eggs	4 minutes
Grade 4–7 eggs	3–3½ minutes

Medium-boiled Eggs Put the eggs in a saucepan and cover them with cold water; bring to the boil over low heat. As soon as the water boils, remove the pan from the heat, cover it with a lid and leave the eggs to stand for the necessary times:

Grade 1 eggs	6½ minutes
Grade 2 and 3 eggs	6 minutes
Grade 4–7 eggs	4–5 minutes

Hard-boiled Eggs Cook the eggs in boiling water for the recommended times. Plunge them immediately in cold water to prevent further cooking and to make shelling easier. Tap the edges round the middle of the egg with the back of a knife, and pull away the two half-shells.

Grade 1 eggs	12 minutes
Grade 2 and 3 eggs	11 minutes
Grade 4–7 eggs	10 minutes

Frying Eggs

Melt a knob of butter or margarine (25–50 g/1–2 oz is sufficient for 4 eggs) in a frying pan over a low heat. Break the eggs, one by one, on to a saucer and slide them into the fat. Reduce the heat immediately and baste the eggs with the fat to ensure even cooking. Fry the eggs for 3–5 minutes, or until the whites are firm.

Poaching Eggs

Fill a heavy-based frying pan with cold water to a depth of 2.5 cm/1 inch, add a pinch of salt and bring to the boil, reduce the heat and keep the water just simmering. Break the eggs, one by one, on to a saucer and slide them carefully into the gently simmering water.

Using two spoons, quickly and carefully gather the whites over and round the yolks. Then cover the pan with a lid and cook the eggs for 4–5 minutes, or until the yolk is set and the white is firm.

For more regularly-shaped poached eggs, round pastry cutters may be set in the bottom of the pan and the eggs slid inside them. Alternatively, an egg poacher can be used; half fill the pan of the poacher with water, bring to the boil, then reduce the heat and keep the water simmering. Melt a knob of butter or margarine into each egg container and break an egg into them. Season; cover and cook for 2 minutes until set.

Scrambled Eggs

Use two Grade 2 eggs per person, and for each egg allow 15 g/½ oz butter or margarine and 1 tablespoon cream or top of the milk. Beat the eggs with a little salt and freshly ground pepper in a bowl. Melt the butter in a heavy-based pan or in the top of a double boiler, pour in the egg mixture and cook over low heat. As the mixture thickens, stir continuously until soft.

Remove the pan from the heat and stir in the cream or milk.

Baking Eggs

Melt 15 g/½ oz butter in a small ovenproof dish, break an egg into a cup and slide it into the dish. Season lightly with salt and freshly ground pepper. Bake in the centre of a preheated moderate oven (180°C, 350°F, Gas Mark 4) for 7–10 minutes or until the white is just set. Serve immediately.

Omelettes

There are three types of omelette – the French or plain omelette which is light, golden and plump, the English or soufflé omelette which is very fluffy, and the Spanish or tortilla omelette which is flat like a thick pancake.

The French is the most popular and easiest to prepare:

Gently heat an omelette pan. With a fork lightly beat the eggs (about 2–3 per person) with cold water (about 1 teaspoon per egg) and salt and pepper to taste. Put a little butter in the pan, raise the heat and when sizzling (but not brown), pour in the eggs. With a fork or spatula, draw the mixture from the sides to the middle of the pan so that the uncooked egg can run on to the hot pan and set. Repeat until all the egg is lightly cooked – about 1 minute. With the top still runny, fold one-half of the omelette over – the half nearest the handle of the pan. Holding the handle with your palm uppermost, shake the omelette to the edge of the pan and tip on to a warmed plate. Serve at once.

To Cook Long-grain Rice

Long-grain rice makes a splendid meal accompaniment instead of potatoes or pasta and can also be used to make stuffings, savoury salads and gratin-style main meals when mixed with meat, fish, eggs, cheese or vegetables.

For basic cooking of long-grain rice, allow 2 teacups long-grain rice for four people. Place 4 teacups water in a pan with ½ teaspoon salt. Bring to the boil, add the rice, stir well, bring to the boil again, reduce the heat, cover and simmer for 15 minutes. By the end of the cooking time the rice grains will have absorbed the liquid and be fluffy and separate. Stir with a fork to fluff up the rice and serve.

If the rice is of the American easy-cook or par-boiled variety then use 5 teacups of water to 2 teacups rice and cook for 20 minutes.

To Cook Pasta

For basic cooking of pasta, allow 50 g/2 oz per person. Cook each 100 g/4 oz pasta in at least 1.2 litres/2 pints water.

Place the water and salt to taste in a saucepan and bring to the boil. Add the pasta, stir briskly, bring to the boil and cook for the time stated on the packet instructions. Drain and serve.

To Make a Basic White Coating Sauce

25 g	butter	1 oz
25 g	plain flour	1 oz
300 ml	milk	½ pint
	salt and pepper	

1. Melt the butter in a saucepan. Remove from the heat and stir in the flour.
2. Return to the heat and cook gently for 2–3 minutes – this is called cooking the roux. Do not allow to brown and stir frequently.
3. Remove from the heat and gradually add the milk, blending well to keep the sauce smooth.
4. Return to the heat and bring to the boil, stirring constantly. Continue stirring while the mixture boils for about 1 minute.
5. Add salt and pepper to taste and use as required. **Makes 300 ml/½ pint**

Variations

Basic White Pouring Sauce Prepare as above but use 15 g/½ oz butter and 15 g/½ oz plain flour to 300 ml/½ pint milk.

Cheese Sauce Add 50 g/2 oz grated cheese and a pinch of mustard powder with the salt and pepper. Stir well to melt the cheese.

Parsley Sauce Add 1 tablespoon chopped parsley to the sauce with the salt and pepper. Stir well to blend.

Onion Sauce Add 100 g/4 oz chopped cooked onion to the sauce with the salt and pepper. Stir well to blend.

Curry Sauce Prepare as above, adding 4 tablespoons very finely chopped onion, 2 teaspoons curry powder (strength according to taste) and ¾ teaspoon sugar with the flour. Just before serving stir in 1 teaspoon lemon juice.

Roasting Meat and Poultry

Roasting meat and poultry isn't a difficult task although you could be forgiven for thinking so. Simply remember that lean cuts of meat need spreading with melted butter or cooking fat before cooking and that to calculate cooking times you must weigh the joint after it has been stuffed or prepared in any way.

Either place the joint in a special roasting bag or place in a roasting tin and cover lightly with foil. Remember *not* to cover pork or duck since the skin here needs to crisp.

Preheat the oven to moderate (180°C, 350°F, Gas Mark 4) and add the meat. Cook for the following times:

Beef Allow 20–25 minutes per 450 g/1 lb and 20 minutes over.
Pork and Veal Allow 30–35 minutes per 450 g/1 lb and 35 minutes over.
Lamb Allow 25–30 minutes per 450 g/1 lb and 30 minutes over.
Poultry and Game Allow 20–25 minutes per 450 g/1 lb and 25 minutes over.

To Make a Gravy

1–1½ tablespoons	plain flour	1–1½ tablespoons
300 ml	stock	½ pint

1. Remove the roast joint from the roasting pan and place on a warmed serving plate.
2. Spoon away all of the fat from the pan except for 1 tablespoon. Leave any pieces of meat residue – they will add flavour.
3. Stir in the flour, according to the thickness of gravy you require, blending well.
4. Gradually add the stock, blending well. Return to the heat and cook gently, stirring constantly, until the mixture thickens. Pour into a warmed sauceboat and serve. If there is a lot of meat sediment then you may like to strain the gravy into the sauceboat. Serve hot. **Makes 300 ml/½ pint**

Basic Vegetable Cooking

There is a vegetable to suit every main meal dish and a different one in season during every month of the year. Cooking instructions vary enormously – check the chart below for first class results.

For boiling vegetables, bring the water to the boil, add a little salt and the vegetables. Cook for the recommended times. Always use the minimum amount of water, just about enough to cover.

Vegetable	Preparation	Cooking Time in Minutes
Asparagus	Remove the woody base of the stems, tie in a bundle and stand upright in the saucepan, tips at the top, to boil.	25–30
Aubergines	Slice thinly, dégorge (see page 40) and fry in hot oil and butter.	15–20
Beans – Broad	Shell and boil.	10–15
– French	Top and tail and boil. Use minimum time for very thin French beans.	8–15
– Runner	Top and tail and trim sides. Slice thinly and boil.	10–15
Beetroot	Wash and trim. Boil in skins then cool and remove. Slice to serve fresh in a sauce or in spiced vinegar.	50–90
Broccoli	Trim stems or florets to an even size and boil.	10–12
Brussels Sprouts	Trim the base and remove any outer damaged leaves. Boil.	6–8
Cabbage and Greens	Slice into quarters or shred and boil.	3–6
Carrots	Peel or scrape, slice if liked and boil.	15–20
Cauliflower	Divide and trim into florets. Boil.	8–10
Celery	Boil whole or sliced. For best results cook in flavoured stock.	10–15
Corn on the Cob	Remove husk and silk threads and boil.	10–12
Courgettes	Top and tail, slice if liked then boil.	6–8
Leeks	Wash very well and slice before boiling.	12–15
Mushrooms	Wipe and leave whole or slice. Cook in a little butter.	4–6
Onions	Peel and slice or chop then fry in butter. Add to other vegetables for flavour.	5
Parsnips	Peel and quarter, slice or chop. Boil then roast with joint.	15
Peas	Shell and boil.	8–12
Potatoes – Old	Peel and boil. Roast, bake or fry.	20–25
	Also bake in their jackets.	90–120
– New	Scrub or scrape and boil.	20–25
Spinach	Wash and cook only in water clinging to the leaves.	8–10
Swedes	Peel, chop and boil. Top or mash with butter to serve.	30
Tomatoes	Fry lightly in butter, use raw or stuff and bake.	
Turnips	Peel, chop and boil. Top or mash with butter to serve.	30

Centre left, Basic Victoria Sandwich (page 17); *bottom right*, Scones (page 17); *top*, how to line a flan tin before baking "blind" (page 32).

Yorkshire Pudding

100 g	plain flour	4 oz
	salt	
1	egg	1
300 ml	milk	½ pint
1 tablespoon	water	1 tablespoon
50 g	butter or meat drippings	2 oz

1. Preheat the oven to hot (220°C, 425°F, Gas Mark 7).
2. Sift the flour and a large pinch of salt into a bowl, make a well in the middle and add the egg. Gradually stir the flour into the egg, adding the milk to keep the mixture smooth and liquid. Beat very well then stir in the water.
3. Leave to stand for 30 minutes.
4. Place the butter or drippings in one large 25 × 30-cm/10 × 12-inch baking tin or divide between 12 small Yorkshire pudding tins. Place in the oven and heat until a haze just appears.
5. Remove and carefully add the batter. Return to the oven, just above centre, and cook the large pudding for 30 minutes and the smaller for 10 minutes.
6. Reduce the oven temperature to moderately hot (200°C, 400°F, Gas Mark 6) and cook the large pudding for a further 15–20 minutes and the smaller puddings for a further 5–10 minutes. Serve at once. **Serves 6–8**

Basic Rice Pudding

3 tablespoons	short or round-grain rice	3 tablespoons
600 ml	milk	1 pint
1	vanilla pod	1
25 g	caster sugar	1 oz
150 ml	double cream	¼ pint

1. Place the rice, milk, vanilla pod and sugar in a heavy-based saucepan. Bring to the boil, lower the heat, cover and cook very gently for 1½ hours until tender, stirring occasionally.
2. Alternatively bring to the boil then place in an ovenproof dish. Cook in a preheated cool oven (150°C, 300°F, Gas Mark 2) for 2 hours.
3. Remove the vanilla pod and allow to cool slightly.
4. Whip the cream in a bowl until it stands in soft peaks. Fold into the rice mixture with a metal spoon.
5. Serve warm or cold. **Serves 4**

Shortcrust Pastry

Many recipes call for shortcrust pastry and will often specify a weight required. If for example 175 g/6 oz shortcrust pastry is required then this means pastry made using 175 g/6 oz flour. If 225 g/8 oz shortcrust pastry is called for then this would be pastry made using 225 g/8 oz flour. The weight always refers to the quantity of flour used. And remember that you always use half the quantity of fat to flour when making pastry.

175 g	plain flour	6 oz
	pinch of salt	
40 g	butter	1½ oz
40 g	lard	1½ oz
2 tablespoons	iced water	2 tablespoons

1. Sift the flour and salt into a mixing bowl. Cut the butter and lard into small pieces and toss in the flour lightly.
2. Rub the fats into the flour with your fingertips until the mixture resembles fine breadcrumbs.
3. Add the water, sprinkling it over the rubbed in mixture, and bind with a round-bladed knife and then the fingertips to a firm but pliable dough.
4. Turn on to a lightly floured surface and knead lightly until smooth and free from cracks. Use as required. If not for immediate use then wrap in cling film and chill in the refrigerator until required. **Makes 175 g/6 oz**

Special Custard Sauce

Custard sauce can be made quickly and easily using custard powder. When you have the time it is really worth the effort to make a true custard sauce using egg yolks, milk and sugar.

2	egg yolks	2
15 g	caster sugar	½ oz
2 drops	vanilla essence	2 drops
300 ml	milk	½ pint

1. Place the egg yolks in a bowl and beat until creamy.
2. Place the sugar, vanilla essence and milk in a saucepan and heat until hot but not boiling. Add to the egg yolks, whisking all the time.
3. Place the bowl over a saucepan of hot but *not* boiling water and cook, stirring continuously, until the custard coats the back of the spoon, about 20–25 minutes.
4. Pour into a warmed jug and serve hot. **Makes 300 ml/½ pint**

Scones
(Illustrated on page 15)

225 g	plain flour	8 oz
1 tablespoon	baking powder	1 tablespoon
½ teaspoon	salt	½ teaspoon
50 g	butter	2 oz
25 g	caster sugar	1 oz
150 ml	milk	¼ pint
	milk to glaze	

1. Preheat the oven to hot (220°C, 425°F, Gas Mark 7).
2. Sift the flour, baking powder and salt into a bowl.
3. Rub in the butter with your fingertips until the mixture resembles fine breadcrumbs.
4. Stir in the sugar and milk and mix to a soft but manageable dough with a fork. Turn on to a lightly floured surface and knead until smooth.
5. Roll out on a lightly floured surface with a floured rolling pin to about 1 cm/½ inch thick. Stamp out 12 rounds using a 5-cm/2-inch scone or biscuit cutter, re-rolling where necessary.
6. Place the rounds on a greased baking tray and brush with a little milk to glaze. Bake in the oven for 8–10 minutes until well risen and golden brown. Cool on a wire rack.
7. Split and serve with butter or whipped cream and jam. For Fruit Scones, prepare as above but add 40g/1½ oz currants or sultanas with the sugar.
Makes 12

Basic Victoria Sandwich
(Illustrated on page 15)

125 g	butter	4 oz
125 g	caster sugar	4 oz
2	eggs, beaten	2
125 g	self-raising flour, sifted	4 oz
3 tablespoons	jam	3 tablespoons
150 ml	double cream, whipped	¼ pint
	sifted icing sugar to dust	

1. Preheat the oven to moderate (180°C, 350°F, Gas Mark 4).
2. Place the butter and sugar in a mixing bowl and cream, with a wooden spoon, until light and fluffy.
3. Beat in the eggs with a little of the flour to prevent the mixture curdling. Carefully fold in the remaining flour with a metal spoon.
4. Divide the mixture between two greased and base-lined 18-cm/7-inch sandwich tins and level the tops with a palette knife.
5. Bake in the oven for 25–30 minutes or until the tops spring back when lightly touched with the fingertips. Leave to cool in the tins for 2–3 minutes then transfer to a wire rack to cool completely.
6. When cold, spread the jam over one of the cake layers and top with the whipped cream. Cover with the second cake. Dust the top with a little sifted icing sugar.
7. Cut into wedges to serve. **Serves 6**

Basic White Bread

1 tablespoon	dried yeast	1 tablespoon
1 teaspoon	caster sugar	1 teaspoon
100 ml	warm water	3½ fl oz
100 ml	warm milk	3½ fl oz
400 g	strong plain white flour	14 oz
2 teaspoons	salt	2 teaspoons
25 g	butter	1 oz
	beaten egg to glaze	

1. Place the yeast, sugar, water and milk in a jug. Mix well to blend. Leave in a warm place until frothy, about 15 minutes.
2. Sift the flour and salt into a large mixing bowl. Rub in the butter with your fingertips.
3. Add the yeast liquid and mix to a smooth dough. Turn out on to a lightly floured surface and knead until smooth and elastic, about 10 minutes. To knead press the dough into a flat shape, stretching and pushing it as you do so. Then roll it into a ball again and repeat the stretching and pulling action until the dough feels smooth and silky.
4. Place in an oiled bowl and cover with cling film. Leave to rise in a warm place until doubled in size. This can take anything from 1–1½ hours, depending on the temperature of the room.
5. Turn the dough on to a lightly floured surface and knead again to release the air bubbles – this is called knocking back the dough.
6. Flatten the dough out to an oblong about 2.5 cm/1 inch thick. Fold in three and tuck the ends over the seam. Place, seam side down, in a greased 900-g/2-lb loaf tin. Cover with cling film and leave to rise again for about 1 hour.
7. Meanwhile preheat the oven to hot (220°C, 425°F, Gas Mark 7).
8. Remove the cling film and brush the loaf with beaten egg to glaze. Bake in the oven for 35–40 minutes.
9. When cooked the loaf should sound hollow when removed from the tin and rapped on the bottom with the knuckles. Allow to cool on a wire rack.
Makes 1 (900-g/2-lb) loaf

BETTER BREAKFASTS

Crunchy Muesli
(Illustrated opposite)

Muesli became world famous after it had been adapted and used as part of a health diet in a well-known clinic in Switzerland – before that it was just a simple Swiss peasant dish. Change the balance of the ingredients occasionally for a different result.

225 g	wholewheat flakes	8 oz
225 g	rye flakes	8 oz
225 g	porridge oats	8 oz
225 g	barley or bran flakes	8 oz
350 g	mixed roasted nuts	12 oz
450 g	mixed dried fruit (apples, pears, currants, sultanas, apricots and prunes, for example)	1 lb
225 g	raisins	8 oz

1. Place all the ingredients in a large bowl and mix very well to blend.
2. Spoon into a large airtight tin or plastic bag and cover or secure. Store in a cool, dry place.
3. Serve 2–3 tablespoons per portion with milk, cream, yogurt or fruit juice. **Makes 2 kg/4¼ lb**

Orange Sunrise
(Illustrated opposite)

Occasionally there is hardly any time at all for breakfast – that's when this meal in a glass is just the order of the day!

150 ml	unsweetened orange juice	¼ pint
1	egg	1
	dash of lemon juice	

1. Beat the orange juice with the egg until frothy. This is easiest done in a blender goblet for just a few seconds.
2. Stir in a dash of lemon juice. Pour into a glass and serve. **Serves 1**

Breakfast Fruit Salad
(Illustrated opposite)

This is a delicious breakfast dish that can be served hot or cold. Serve topped with yogurt or soured cream if liked.

75 g	dried prunes	3 oz
75 g	dried apricots	3 oz
50 g	raisins	2 oz
3	bananas, peeled and thickly sliced	3
25 g	clear honey	1 oz
	grated rind of ½ lemon	
25 g	butter	1 oz
200 ml	unsweetened orange juice	7 fl oz

1. Soak the prunes and apricots overnight in cold water then drain.
2. Preheat the oven to moderate (180°C, 350°F, Gas Mark 4).
3. Place the prunes, apricots, raisins and bananas in an ovenproof dish. Dissolve the honey in a little hot water and pour over the fruit mixture.
4. Sprinkle with the lemon rind and dot with the butter. Cover and bake for 35 minutes.
5. Add the orange juice, blending well. Cover and cook for a further 5 minutes. Serve hot or cold. **Serves 4**

Special Feature

Soured Cream

Soured cream is not cream that has gone sour but cultured cream that has a piquant, refreshing taste and smooth texture.

If soured cream is unavailable then it is possible to make a good substitute by blending 150 ml/¼ pint double cream with 2–3 teaspoons lemon juice.

Left, Breakfast Fruit Salad (opposite); *top*, Pear Muesli with Yogurt (page 20); *top right*, Orange Sunrise (opposite), *bottom right*, Crunchy Muesli (opposite).

Pear Muesli with Yogurt
(Illustrated on page 19)

This is a hearty yet refreshing breakfast dish best made just before serving.

1	dessert pear	1
2 teaspoons	lemon juice	2 teaspoons
3 tablespoons	natural yogurt	3 tablespoons
1 teaspoon	honey	1 teaspoon
1½ tablespoons	water	1½ tablespoons
25 g	muesli	1 oz
7–15 g	almonds, chopped	¼–½ oz

1. Core the pear and chop finely without peeling.
2. Place in a serving bowl, sprinkle with the lemon juice and mix well to prevent the pear from turning brown.
3. Add the yogurt, honey and water and mix well.
4. Stir in the muesli, tossing well to coat. Sprinkle with the almonds and serve at once. **Serves 1**

Honeyed Prunes

Prunes are doubly delicious if they are first soaked in fruit juice and then cooked with a little honey. Serve with yogurt or cereal if liked.

6–8	prunes	6–8
150 ml	unsweetened orange or grapefruit juice	¼ pint
½ teaspoon	clear honey	½ teaspoon

1. Place the prunes in a saucepan with the fruit juice. Cover and leave to soak overnight.
2. Bring to the boil, lower the heat and simmer gently for 5 minutes, adding a little more fruit juice if required.
3. Remove from the heat, stir in the honey and serve while still warm. **Serves 1**

Supreme Scrambled Eggs

This is a tasty family-style late breakfast or brunch dish made with sausages, scrambled eggs, sweetcorn and cheese. Serve with freshly made toast fingers.

25 g	butter	1 oz
225 g	skinless pork sausages, cut into 1-cm/½-inch pieces	8 oz
1	onion, peeled and chopped	1
1 (312-g) can	cream-style sweetcorn	1 (11-oz) can
4	eggs, beaten	4
	salt and pepper	
1 tablespoon	chopped parsley	1 tablespoon
50 g	cheese, grated	2 oz

1. Preheat the grill to moderately hot.
2. Place the butter in a frying pan and heat to melt. Add the sausages and onion and cook until lightly browned on all sides, about 5 minutes.
3. Stir in the cream-style corn and mix well to blend.
4. Stir in the eggs, salt and pepper to taste and parsley, blending well. Cook over a gentle heat, stirring frequently, until the egg mixture is lightly scrambled. Spoon into a flameproof serving dish and sprinkle with the cheese.
5. Cook under the grill until the cheese is golden and bubbly. Serve at once with hot toast fingers. **Serves 4**

Grilled Citrus Start

Grapefruit makes delicious breakfast time eating, and this recipe combines sharp grapefruit segments with orange juice and sugar.

2 large	grapefruit	2 large
6 tablespoons	unsweetened orange juice	6 tablespoons
2–3 tablespoons	demerara sugar	2–3 tablespoons

1. Using a grapefruit knife, remove the flesh from the grapefruit halves in segments, keeping the shells intact.
2. Cut the segments into bite-sized pieces and return to the grapefruit shells.
3. Mix the orange juice with the sugar and spoon over the grapefruit.
4. Cook under a hot grill for about 5 minutes or until hot and bubbly. Serve at once. **Serves 4**

Kipper Toasts

Why not try something fishy for a change at breakfast time – this recipe combines kippers with cream and seasonings. Serve on slices of toast or fried bread.

350 g	kipper fillets	12 oz
25 g	butter	1 oz
	salt and pepper	
2–3 tablespoons	cream or top of the milk	2–3 tablespoons
4	slices toast or fried bread	4
1	lemon, quartered to garnish	1

1. Place the kipper fillets in a deep frying pan with a little boiling water to just cover. Cover and simmer for 5 minutes until tender.
2. Drain well and flake into a bowl, removing and discarding any bones.
3. Melt the butter in a saucepan, add the flaked kipper and salt and pepper to taste. Cook until just hot.
4. Add the cream or milk and reheat until piping hot.
5. Spoon on to the toast or fried bread and serve at once garnished with the lemon quarters.
Serves 4

Creamy Porridge

Porridge oats are generally available in two varieties – the traditional slow-cooking type and the quick-cooking rolled oats variety. Both should be cooked in water or a mixture of water and milk for good results (do look at the packet instructions). The recipe below uses the quick-cooking type of oats and is perfect for serving on cold winter mornings.

175 ml	water	6 fl oz
175 ml	milk	6 fl oz
$\frac{1}{2}$ teaspoon	salt	$\frac{1}{2}$ teaspoon
65 g	quick-cooking porridge oats	$2\frac{1}{2}$ oz

1. Place the water, milk, salt and porridge oats in a saucepan.
2. Bring to the boil, stirring constantly so that the porridge cooks and thickens smoothly. Reduce the heat and simmer for 5–8 minutes until very creamy.
3. Spoon into deep serving bowls and serve while still hot, with sugar if liked. **Serves 2**

Marrow, Rhubarb and Ginger Jam

Homemade jam is unbeatable and this one is made with marrow and rhubarb. It makes a tasty change at breakfast time from the usual pot of marmalade.

1.5 kg	hard yellow marrow	3 lb
1.5 kg	rhubarb	3 lb
3 kg	sugar	6 lb
75 g	preserved ginger	3 oz
3	lemons	3

1. Skin and cube the marrow. Trim and cut the rhubarb into short lengths. Layer the rhubarb, marrow and sugar in a large mixing bowl. Cover and leave overnight.
2. Place in a large saucepan or preserving pan with the chopped ginger.
3. Carefully cut away the rind from the lemons and squeeze the juice. Add the juice to the rhubarb mixture and place the rind in a piece of muslin. Add to the pan, bring to the boil and boil for about 30 minutes, until the jam reaches setting point (see page below).
4. Remove and discard the lemon rind. Spoon the jam into warm sterilised jars, cover, seal, label and store in a cool dry place until required.
Makes 5.5 kg/12 lb

Special Feature

Testing the Setting Point of Jam

The best way to check if the setting point has been reached in jams and jellies is to place a little of the mixture on a cool saucer. Allow to cool then push the mixture with the finger. If the surface wrinkles, setting point has been reached. If the surface does not wrinkle then cook longer.

Left, Spaghetti and Bacon Omelette (opposite); *top*, Bacon Nesting Eggs (opposite); *bottom right*, Kedgeree (opposite).

Kedgeree
(Illustrated opposite)

Kedgeree is a rice and fish dish of Indian origin that is delicious served at breakfast or brunch.

225 g	long-grain rice	8 oz
	salt and pepper	
50 g	butter	2 oz
450 g	cold cooked smoked haddock, skinned and flaked	1 lb
2	eggs, beaten	2
1 tablespoon	milk	1 tablespoon
	chopped parsley to garnish	

1. Cook the rice in boiling salted water according to the packet instructions, about 15–20 minutes. Drain thoroughly.
2. Place in a large deep frying pan and stir in the butter until melted. Add the haddock, eggs and milk, blending well. Cook over a gentle heat for about 10 minutes until the egg has lightly set, stirring frequently. Add salt and pepper to taste.
3. Pile on to a warmed serving dish and sprinkle with chopped parsley. Serve at once. **Serves 4–6**

Bacon Nesting Eggs
(Illustrated opposite)

These attractive one-pot breakfast dishes are simply baked eggs nesting in a mixture of bacon, breadcrumbs and cheese – but they give the impression that you have been in the kitchen for hours!

40 g	butter	1½ oz
25 g	fresh white breadcrumbs	1 oz
4	rashers streaky bacon, rinded	4
50 g	cheese, grated	2 oz
4	eggs	4
	salt and pepper	

1. Preheat the oven to moderately hot (200°C, 400°F, Gas Mark 6).
2. Place 25 g/1 oz of the butter in a frying pan and heat to melt. Add the breadcrumbs and fry, stirring frequently, until golden. Remove and drain on absorbent kitchen paper.
3. Meanwhile, lightly grill or partially fry the bacon rashers until barely cooked. Line the sides of four ramekin (small ovenproof) dishes with the bacon.
4. Mix the breadcrumbs with the cheese and spoon into the base of the ramekins. Carefully crack an egg into each dish and season with salt and pepper to taste.
5. Dot with the remaining butter, place the ramekins on a baking tray and cook in the oven for about 7–8 minutes until the eggs are just set. Serve at once, garnished if preferred. **Serves 4**

Spaghetti and Bacon Omelette
(Illustrated opposite)

What could be nicer at breakfast time than combining popular eggs and bacon with tasty spaghetti in tomato sauce? Cut this omelette into portions depending upon size of appetite!

2	rashers streaky bacon, rinded and chopped	2
1 (425-g) can	wholewheat spaghetti in tomato sauce	1 (15-oz) can
4	eggs	4
2 tablespoons	water	2 tablespoons
	salt and pepper	
25 g	butter	1 oz

1. Place the bacon in a pan and cook until crispy, about 5 minutes. Drain on absorbent kitchen paper.
2. Meanwhile, place the spaghetti in a saucepan and heat through until hot.
3. Break the eggs into a bowl. Add the water and salt and pepper to taste, beating well to blend.
4. Melt the butter in a medium non-stick or 'seasoned' omelette or frying pan. Add the egg mixture and cook over a fairly high heat until the eggs have set very slightly at the bottom of the omelette. Using a flat-bladed knife, gently pull the egg away from the sides of the pan, allowing the unset egg to run to the sides. Continue cooking this way until the omelette is set and the underside is golden.
5. Spread the spaghetti over one half of the omelette. Using a fish slice or spatula fold the remaining half of the omelette over the spaghetti to enclose. Divide into portions, slip on to warmed plates and serve at once sprinkled with the bacon.

Serves 2–3

SIZZLING SNACKS

Super Macaroni Cheese

Macaroni cheese has been a favourite snack or supper dish for many years and now is made all the more mouth-watering by adding onion, eggs and bacon.

25 g	butter	1 oz
1	onion, peeled and chopped	1
3	hard-boiled eggs, shelled	3
2 (425-g) cans	macaroni cheese	2 (15-oz) cans
	or 250 g/9 oz cooked macaroni mixed with 300 ml/½ pint cheese sauce (see page 13)	
	salt and pepper	
6 small	rashers bacon, rinded and grilled	6 small
75 g	cheese, grated	3 oz

1. Preheat the grill to moderately hot.
2. Place the butter in a large frying pan and heat gently to melt. Add the onion and fry for 3 minutes.
3. Coarsely chop two of the eggs on a board with a knife. Add to the onion with the macaroni cheese or macaroni and cheese sauce, and salt and pepper to taste. Cook gently to heat through.
4. Spoon into a flameproof dish. Top with the grilled bacon and the remaining egg cut into slices. Sprinkle with the cheese.
5. Place under the grill and cook until golden and bubbly. Serve piping hot. **Serves 4–6**

Special Feature

Several types of oils have been used in the recipes in this book since each oil has its own character, colour, flavour and purpose.

As a general guide, use corn oil or a vegetable blend for cooking when flavour comes second to oil stability at high temperatures; walnut, safflower, grape seed and olive oil for salads and dressings when flavour and lightness are all important; peanut or groundnut and sunflower for both cooking and salads; and sesame seed for salads or stir-frying Chinese-style dishes when a distinctive flavour is required.

Mexican Spaghetti Supper

Mexican food is typically spicy and often includes peppers, chilli powder and tomatoes. This is a simple recipe to make using canned spaghetti in tomato sauce with peppers and chilli powder – serve it with hot crusty bread and salad for a hearty snack or supper dish.

4 tablespoons	oil	4 tablespoons
1 large	onion, peeled and finely chopped	1 large
450 g	lean minced beef	1 lb
2 teaspoons	chilli powder	2 teaspoons
	salt and pepper	
1 large	green pepper, cored, seeded and cut into strips	1 large
150 ml	beef stock	¼ pint
1 (425-g) can	spaghetti in tomato sauce	1 (15-oz) can
3 tablespoons	soured cream (optional)	3 tablespoons

1. Heat the oil in a large lidded frying pan until hot. Add the onion and cook gently for 3 minutes.
2. Add the minced beef and cook until lightly browned, stirring occasionally.
3. Add the chilli powder, salt and pepper to taste, green pepper strips and stock. Mix well to blend. Cover and cook over a gentle heat for 20 minutes.
4. Add the spaghetti in tomato sauce and cook for a further 2 minutes, stirring well.
5. Swirl the soured cream over the top of the pasta and mince mixture, if liked. Serve at once. **Serves 4**

Special Feature

Eating Long Pasta

Many people would prefer to eat spaghetti or long macaroni in the privacy of their own homes, rather than attempting it in public!

The best way is to stick your fork into the long pasta, and twist it until a manageable mouthful is wound around the fork. Lift the fork and pop it into your mouth, biting off any trailing strands and letting them drop back on to your plate.

Savoury Spicy Pancakes

Shrove Tuesday is the day when the whole of Britain seems to eat pancakes. The custom originates from the time when housewives had to use up their eggs and milk before the Lent fast started, and so made pancakes.

In Olney in Buckinghamshire, they still hold the famous Pancake Race – this race is believed to have started back in the 15th Century when a housewife in her eagerness not to be late for church after hearing the bell ring, rushed out of her house with frying pan still in hand.

Pancakes eaten on Shrove Tuesday are often flavoured with orange or lemon juice and sprinkled with sugar. Here is a savoury idea that is sure to be just as popular.

	Pancake Batter	
75 g	plain flour	3 oz
$\frac{1}{2}$ teaspoon	salt	$\frac{1}{2}$ teaspoon
1 teaspoon	mustard powder	1 teaspoon
2	eggs	2
150 ml	milk	$\frac{1}{4}$ pint
2 tablespoons	oil	2 tablespoons
	oil for cooking	
	Filling	
40 g	butter	$1\frac{1}{2}$ oz
2	onions, peeled and chopped	2
1 large	green pepper, cored seeded and chopped	1 large
5	tomatoes, peeled, seeded and chopped	5
100 g	mild Cheddar cheese	4 oz
50 g	cooked ham	2 oz
	salt and pepper	
2 teaspoons	chopped parsley	2 teaspoons

1. Place the flour, salt and mustard in a bowl. Make a well in the middle. Add the eggs and gradually stir the flour into the eggs, adding the milk to keep the mixture smooth and liquid. Beat very well then stir in the oil. Cover and leave to stand for 1 hour.
2. When ready to cook, heat a medium-sized frying pan until hot and add a few drops of oil. Pour in about 5 tablespoons of the batter and tilt the pan to coat the bottom evenly. Cook until the underside is brown, then turn over and cook for about 10–15 seconds. Remove the pancake with a fish slice and keep warm on a plate over a saucepan of simmering water. Cover with a large pan lid. Repeat until all the batter has been used up.
3. To make the filling, place the butter in a frying pan and heat to melt. Add the onions and cook until soft, about 5 minutes. Add the pepper and tomatoes and cook for a further 5 minutes.
4. Meanwhile dice the cheese and ham into small cubes. Stir into the hot vegetable mixture with salt and pepper to taste and the parsley and remove from the heat.
5. To serve, place one pancake on a warmed serving dish. Spread with some of the filling. Repeat with the remaining pancakes and filling, ending with a pancake.
6. Serve at once, cutting the pancake stack like a cake, into wedges. **Serves 4–6**

Fishy Jacket Potatoes
(Illustrated on page 27)

Baked potatoes are doubly delicious when the flesh is scooped out, mixed with other savoury ingredients, returned to the skin and baked until crisp and golden.

If you have a microwave oven in your kitchen then this recipe can be made extra fast since you only need to cook the potatoes on FULL POWER for 12–16 minutes, or about 4–6 minutes each, rather than cooking in the conventional oven.

4	potatoes suitable for baking in their jackets	4
100 g	peeled prawns	4 oz
4	spring onions, finely chopped	4
1 tablespoon	snipped chives	1 tablespoon
50 g	butter, softened	2 oz
	salt and pepper	
4 teaspoons	thousand island dressing	4 teaspoons
8	unpeeled prawns to garnish	8

1. Preheat the oven to moderately hot (190°C, 375°F, Gas Mark 5).
2. Wash, scrub and dry the potatoes. Prick well all over with a fork to prevent the potatoes from bursting during cooking. Stand on a baking tray and bake, just above the centre of the oven, for $1\frac{1}{2}$–2 hours, or until the potatoes feel tender when gently pressed.
3. Remove from the oven and slice the top from the flat side of the potato. Scoop out the potato with a teaspoon to within 5 mm/$\frac{1}{4}$ inch of the skin. Place in a bowl and add the peeled prawns, spring onions, chives, butter and salt and pepper to taste. Mix well until thoroughly combined. Spoon back into the potato skins. Place on the baking tray and return to the oven for 10 minutes until golden.
4. Spoon a little of the dressing over the top of each potato and garnish with the unpeeled prawns. Serve at once, on a bed of lettuce if liked. **Serves 4**

Cheesy Oatburgers
(Illustrated opposite)

Cheese is probably one of the most versatile and popular snack foods – not surprising since there are so many varieties to choose from now. Do you know and have you tried many of the great English cheeses? Red Leicester is used in the recipe below but use any one of the other popular types if you prefer (see 'Do You Know the Great English Cheeses').

175 g	Red Leicester cheese	6 oz
1 small	green pepper	1 small
1 large	tomato, peeled and chopped	1 large
1 small	onion, peeled and chopped	1 small
100 g	porridge oats	4 oz
2	eggs	2
	salt and pepper	
2–3 tablespoons	oil for frying	2–3 tablespoons

1. Preheat a grill until moderately hot. Grate the cheese and place 100 g/4 oz in a large bowl. Reserve the remainder for the topping.
2. Core, remove the seeds and finely chop the pepper. Add to the cheese with the tomato, onion and porridge oats.
3. Lightly beat the eggs and add to the cheese mixture with salt and pepper to taste. Mix very well with a wooden spoon until blended.
4. Divide the mixture into four large or six smaller portions and shape each into a flat patty or hamburger.
5. Place the oil in a large frying pan and heat until hot. Carefully add the burgers, using a fish slice. Fry gently until golden brown, about 4–5 minutes. Turn them carefully with a large spatula and cook until golden on the second side, about 4 minutes.
6. Sprinkle the reserved cheese on top of the burgers and transfer to the grill rack. Cook under the grill until golden and bubbly.
7. Serve at once, in soft baps if liked.

Makes 4 large or 6 small burgers

Special Feature

Do You Know the Great English Cheeses?

Cheddar Probably the most popular cheese we eat in Britain. It is a hard cheese with a smooth, even texture and can be mild and creamy tasting or mature and strong.

Stilton Stilton is one of our oldest and most famous cheeses. There are two types – blue and white. Blue is better known because of its veining – made by piercing holes in the cheese during the ripening process to allow air to penetrate and produce the blue mould. White Stilton is a young cheese with an open, crumbly texture. Today, Stilton can only be made in the three shires of Leicester, Nottingham and Derby and its 'recipe' is a closely guarded secret.

Cheshire Cheshire cheese dates back to Roman Britain and is featured in the Domesday Book (compiled between 1084–1085). It is usually white in colour but there are red and blue varieties. It has a characteristic salty tang and open, crumbly texture.

Caerphilly This is the only surviving Welsh cheese and was known as the 'miners'' cheese. It is a white, smooth cheese with a fresh, mild flavour and salty aftertaste.

Lancashire There are two types of Lancashire cheese – double and single curd. Double is rich and creamy, while single is drier and crumbly. It is creamy-white with a mild flavour and is the favourite cheese for toasting.

Wensleydale Wensleydale was originally produced by the monks at Rievaulx Abbey in Yorkshire in the 11th century. It is a mild cheese, slightly flaky in texture. It is creamy white coloured and has a gentle honeyed aftertaste.

Red Leicester This is a highly coloured cheese with a reddish hue produced by adding a natural dye to the cheese process. It is a semi-hard cheese with a softer flakier texture than Cheddar and a clean fresh taste.

Double Gloucester A reddish cheese with rich full taste, smooth creamy texture and fine flavour. It is the cheese still associated with the centuries old custom of cheese rolling on Whit Monday at Cooper's Hill, just outside Gloucester. The ceremony is used to mark the commencement of the old cheese-making season and is generally to greet the spring.

Derby This is a mild, hard, moist cheese with a delicate flavour. It has a variation called Sage Derby which is Derby cheese mixed with fresh sage leaves – producing a cheese with a pleasant green colour and unusual taste.

Bottom, Cheesy Oatburgers (opposite); *top*, Bean Pizza (page 28); *right*, Fishy Jacket Potatoes (page 25).

Leek, Bacon and Tomato Risotto

A risotto is an Italian rice dish where the rice is cooked with lots of tasty ingredients whose flavours it absorbs during cooking. Peeled tomatoes are used in this recipe so it is useful to know how to peel them quickly and in bulk (see below).

450 g	streaky bacon, rinded and chopped	1 lb
4 tablespoons	oil	4 tablespoons
4	leeks, washed and chopped	4
450 g	long-grain rice	1 lb
5	tomatoes, peeled and chopped	5
	salt and pepper	
900 ml	chicken stock	1½ pints
15 g	butter	½ oz
	grated parmesan cheese to sprinkle (optional)	

1. Place the bacon in a large deep frying pan without any extra fat and cook for 6–8 minutes until crisp and golden. Remove the bacon from the pan with a slotted spoon and drain on absorbent kitchen paper.
2. Add the oil to the bacon fat and heat until hot. Add the leeks and cook over a gentle heat for 12 minutes, stirring occasionally.
3. Add the rice and fry for 5 minutes, stirring frequently so that it does not stick. Add the tomatoes and any of their juice, salt and pepper to taste and the stock. Mix well to blend.
4. Bring to the boil, add the bacon, reduce the heat, cover and simmer for 15–20 minutes, stirring occasionally, until the rice is cooked and all the liquid has been absorbed.
5. Spoon into a warmed serving dish and top with the butter. Serve at once, sprinkled with a little grated Parmesan cheese if liked. **Serves 6**

Special Feature

Peeling Tomatoes

You can speedily peel tomatoes in bulk for recipes if you slit the tomato skins with the pointed end of a knife, then cover the tomatoes with boiling water. Leave to stand for 1 minute then drain. The skins will then easily slip away from the flesh for use.

Bean Pizza
(Illustrated on page 27)

Bean Pizza is an easy-to-make recipe for a family snack or supper and it provides an excellent balance of healthy nutrients. In fact, penny for penny, beans offer more protein, calcium, iron and fibre than meat – so this really is a super healthy fast food!

	Base	
225 g	self-raising flour	8 oz
75 g	margarine	3 oz
1	egg, beaten	1
	milk to bind	
	Topping	
2 tablespoons	tomato ketchup	2 tablespoons
2 tablespoons	oil	2 tablespoons
1 large	onion, peeled and chopped	1 large
1	green pepper, cored, seeded and chopped	1
100 g	mushrooms, wiped and sliced	4 oz
1 (450-g) can	baked beans in tomato sauce	1 (15.9-oz) can
1 (227-g) can	frankfurter sausages	1 (8-oz) can
2	tomatoes, sliced	2
100 g	cheese, grated	4 oz

1. Preheat the oven to hot (220°C, 425°F, Gas Mark 7).
2. Sift the flour into a bowl. Rub in the margarine with your fingertips until the mixture resembles fine breadcrumbs. Add the egg and enough milk to mix with a fork to a smooth dough. Knead lightly on a lightly floured surface until smooth and free from cracks.
3. Using a floured rolling pin, roll out the dough on a lightly floured surface to a round about 23 cm/9 inches in diameter. Brush a baking tray generously with oil and lift the pizza base on to the centre of the tray. Brush the tomato ketchup over the dough.
4. To make the topping, place the oil in a pan and heat until hot. Add the onion and fry for about 3 minutes. Add the pepper and mushrooms and fry for a further 2 minutes. Add the beans and mix.
5. Spoon the bean mixture over the pizza base. Drain the frankfurters from the can and arrange on top like the spokes of a wheel. Place the tomato slices in between the frankfurters and sprinkle over the cheese.
6. Bake in the oven for about 20 minutes or until golden brown. Garnish with a sprig of parsley and serve while still hot cut into wedges. **Serves 8**

Mediterranean Omelette

This omelette is called Mediterranean because the peppers, tomatoes and olives used in the recipe are all grown in the Mediterranean in abundance.

50 g	butter	2 oz
1 large	onion, peeled and sliced	1 large
100 g	bacon, rinded and chopped	4 oz
225 g	cooked potatoes, chopped	8 oz
1 small	green pepper, cored, seeded and chopped	1 small
1 small	red pepper, cored, seeded and chopped	1 small
2 small	tomatoes, peeled and chopped	2 small
4	eggs, beaten	4
	salt and pepper	
50 g	cheese, grated	2 oz
6	stuffed green olives, sliced	6

1. Melt the butter in a large heavy-based frying pan. Add the onion and bacon and fry until crisp and lightly browned, about 8–10 minutes.
2. Preheat the grill to moderately hot.
3. Add the potato and peppers to the pan and cook for a further 2 minutes, stirring occasionally. Add the tomatoes and cook for a further 1 minute.
4. Meanwhile, mix the eggs with salt and pepper to taste and pour into the pan. Cook over a gentle heat until the mixture is almost set.
5. Sprinkle with the cheese and olives. Place the omelette, still in the pan, under the grill and cook for about 3 minutes until golden.
6. Serve straight from the pan cut into wedges.

Serves 4

Special Feature

'Seasoning' an Omelette Pan

The success of an omelette can be spoilt if it does not slip easily out of the pan after cooking. The best way to ensure that it does is to 'season' the pan when it is new – 'seasoning' guarantees that omelettes and pancakes will never stick.

To 'season' an omelette pan, simply fill the pan with oil and heat gently. Turn the heat off and leave to stand for 24 hours. Remove the oil and wipe clean with absorbent kitchen paper. Never wash the inside of the pan – simply wipe it clean after use with absorbent kitchen paper.

If the pan should become dirty, rub it with salt, wipe with a damp cloth and oil again lightly.

Ham Club Sandwich

Who invented the club sandwich? No one really seems to know, but one legend has it that a man came home late and hungry from his club one night, raided the refrigerator and made himself a super sandwich which he called 'club'. Another says that the chef of a club made himself a reputation by devising this special sandwich.

The recipe below uses ordinary butter but you could make the sandwich extra tasty by trying one of the flavoured butters below.

3	slices freshly made toast	3
50 g	butter	2 oz
4 small	crisp lettuce leaves	4 small
2 tablespoons	flavoured mayonnaise (curry, lemon or garlic, for example)	2 tablespoons
50 g	cooked ham, sliced	2 oz
1 small	onion, sliced into rings	1 small

1. Spread each slice of toast with the butter.
2. Cover the first slice with the lettuce leaves and mayonnaise.
3. Top with the second slice of toast. Top in turn with the ham and onion rings.
4. Place the third slice of toast on top, buttered side down.
5. Cut the whole sandwich into two triangles to serve.

Serves 1–2

Special Feature

Flavoured Butters

Flavoured butters add interest to sandwiches, grilled foods and savoury dishes, so try making up a batch of them and store in the refrigerator for up to 2 weeks:

Lemon Butter Mix 50 g/2 oz butter with 1 teaspoon finely grated lemon rind and 1 teaspoon lemon juice.

Chive Butter Mix 50 g/2 oz butter with 2 teaspoons snipped chives and 1 teaspoon lemon juice.

Garlic Butter Mix 50 g/2 oz butter with 2 crushed cloves of garlic.

Devilled Butter Mix 50 g/2 oz butter with ½ teaspoon mustard powder, 1 teaspoon Worcestershire sauce, 1 teaspoon lemon juice and salt and pepper to taste.

Souffléed Welsh Rarebit

(Illustrated opposite)

This is a tasty hot snack with a light-as-air cheesy topping.

25 g	butter	1 oz
175 g	cheese, grated	6 oz
2 tablespoons	milk	2 tablespoons
1	egg, separated	1
	made mustard	
	salt and pepper	
4	slices hot toast	4

1. Preheat the grill to moderately hot.
2. Place the butter in a saucepan and melt over a gentle heat.
3. Add the cheese and milk and stir until the cheese has melted and the mixture is smooth.
4. Remove from the heat and stir in the egg yolk, mustard and salt and pepper to taste, blending well.
5. Whisk the egg white in a clean bowl until it stands in stiff peaks. Fold into the cheese mixture with a metal spoon.
6. Spoon the mixture evenly on to the slices of toast. Cook under the grill until the cheese rarebit is puffed up and golden. Serve at once, garnished with a sprig of parsley if liked. **Serves 4**

Special Feature

To Separate Eggs

Knock the egg sharply against the rim of a bowl or cup to break the shell in half. Slip the yolk from one half-shell to the other, until all the white has drained into the bowl. Finally slide the yolk into another bowl.

If any yolk should get into the white, remove it with the edge of the egg shell, a teaspoon or the corner of a piece of absorbent kitchen paper. Even a tiny bit of egg yolk will prevent egg whites from whisking to their full volume, so it is worth taking care when separating eggs.

Union Jack Snack

(Illustrated opposite)

A sandwich is two slices of bread with meat or other relish between, according to the OXFORD DICTIONARY. But who invented the sandwich?

John Montague, fourth Earl of Sandwich, is generally given the credit for 'inventing' the sandwich. While seated at a gaming table and loath to leave it even for food, he called for slices of bread with beef between them to be brought to his table, so that he might continue gaming with one hand while he ate from the other. The Earl's sandwich was doubtless a simple one – he would have been amazed at the size and variety of the triple decker typically British sandwich recipe given below.

4 large	soft round rolls	4 large
75 g	butter	3 oz
100 g	cold roast beef	4 oz
4 tablespoons	mayonnaise	4 tablespoons
1–2 teaspoons	creamed horseradish (optional)	1–2 teaspoons
1 tablespoon	snipped chives	1 tablespoon
4	lettuce leaves	4
100 g	Cheddar cheese	4 oz
1	tomato	1
2 tablespoons	chunky brown pickle	2 tablespoons
1	leek	1
1 tablespoon	raisins	1 tablespoon

1. Using a bread knife, carefully cut three horizontal slits in each roll but do not cut through the bread to the other side. Spread the bread layers with the butter.
2. Slice the roast beef into thin strips and mix with half the mayonnaise, the horseradish relish, if used, and the chives, mixing well.
3. Place a lettuce leaf on the bottom layer of each roll and top with an equal quantity of the beef mixture.
4. Slice the cheese thinly. Fill the middle layer of the rolls with slices of cheese. Slice the tomato thinly and place on top of the cheese. Spoon over a little of the pickle.
5. Wash the leek very well under running water. Using a knife, cut the leek into very thin slices. Place in a bowl and mix with the remaining mayonnaise and the raisins. Use to fill the top layer of the rolls.
6. Press down the top of each roll gently before serving. **Serves 4**

Bottom, Souffléed Welsh Rarebit (opposite); *top*, Union Jack Snack (opposite); *right*, Hot Dogs (page 32).

Hot Dogs
(Illustrated on page 31)

Hot Dogs are one of the simplest but most satisfying snacks around. For variety, try substituting the tomato ketchup with mustard relish, green cucumber chutney or mild piccalilli.

4 large	sausages	4 large
4	long bread rolls or pieces of French bread	4
4 tablespoons	tomato ketchup	4 tablespoons

1. On a chopping board, cut the string of sausages into single links, using scissors.
2. Place the sausages in a dry frying pan on the cooker, over a moderate heat. Fry gently for about 15 minutes, turning frequently to make sure they brown evenly.
3. Place the bread rolls on a board and cut carefully without going right through the bread, leaving it 'hinged' at the back.
4. Using tongs or a fork, place a sausage in each roll. Pour over a little of the tomato ketchup. Serve in soft paper napkins while the sausages are still warm. **Serves 4**

Beef and Orange Risotto

Beef and Orange Risotto is a tasty one-pan meal made with brown rice – use white if you prefer a less nutty flavour.

1 tablespoon	oil	1 tablespoon
300 g	rump steak, cut into thin strips	10 oz
1	onion, peeled and chopped	1
100 g	mushrooms, quartered	4 oz
225 g	brown rice	8 oz
300 ml	beef stock	$\frac{1}{2}$ pint
450 ml	unsweetened orange juice	$\frac{3}{4}$ pint
2 tablespoons	Worcestershire sauce	2 tablespoons
2 tablespoons	tomato purée	2 tablespoons
	salt and pepper	

1. Heat the oil in a large saucepan. Add the steak and fry until browned. Stir in the onion, mushrooms and rice. Cook for 1 minute.
2. Add the beef stock and orange juice. Bring to the boil, reduce the heat, cover and simmer for 25 minutes.
3. Add the Worcestershire sauce, tomato purée and salt and pepper to taste, blending well. Cover and cook for a further 5–10 minutes or until all the liquid has been absorbed and the rice is tender. Serve hot. **Serves 4.**

Tuna Fish Flan

It is necessary to bake this flan 'blind' before adding the filling to ensure that it has a crisp base (see below).

175 g	shortcrust pastry (see page 16)	6 oz
1 (198-g) can	tuna fish, drained	1 (7-oz) can
$\frac{1}{2}$	onion, peeled and grated	$\frac{1}{2}$
2 teaspoons	dried mixed herbs	2 teaspoons
3	eggs	3
300 ml	milk	$\frac{1}{2}$ pint
	salt and pepper	
	tomato and cucumber slices to garnish	

1. Preheat the oven to moderately hot (200°C, 400°F, Gas Mark 6).
2. Roll out the pastry on a lightly floured surface to a round large enough to line the inside of a 20-cm/8-inch flan tin or quiche dish. Lift by rolling the pastry loosely around the rolling pin then lay it over the flan tin and let it unroll. Ease the pastry carefully into the corners of the tin, taking care not to stretch. Roll the rolling pin over the pastry to cut off the excess around the edges. Pinch the edges slightly at the top, raising the pastry above the edge to allow for shrinkage.
3. Bake 'blind' in the oven for 15 minutes.
4. Meanwhile, place the flaked tuna in a bowl with the onion and herbs. Beat the eggs with the milk and add to the tuna mixture. Season to taste with salt and pepper and mix well.
5. Pour into the partially baked flan case, reduce the oven temperature to 190°C, 375°F, Gas Mark 5 and cook for about 30 minutes, until the filling is well risen and firm to the touch.
6. Serve warm or cold cut into wedges. **Serves 4**

Special Feature
To Bake 'Blind'

It is a good idea to bake a flan or quiche 'blind' before adding the filling since it prevents the bottom crust from being undercooked.

To bake 'blind', cut a square of foil or greaseproof paper slightly larger than the flan tin and use it to line the base and sides of the pastry-lined dish. Weigh down with dried beans, or rice if greaseproof paper is used. Cook in a preheated moderately hot oven (200°C, 400°F, Gas Mark 6) for 10–15 minutes. Remove the foil or paper and beans and cook for a further 5 minutes. Add the filling then follow the recipe instructions.

If a completely baked pastry case is required for a recipe then bake for a further 15 minutes after removing the foil or paper and beans.

Herby Mushroom and Pâté Toasted Sandwiches

Grilled or toasted sandwiches make ideal meals or snacks and will adequately cater for one or a crowd.

8	slices white or brown bread, buttered	8
100 g	mild pâté	4 oz
4 teaspoons	chopped mixed herbs, as liked	4 teaspoons
	salt and pepper	
100 g	mushrooms, sliced and cooked in a little butter	4 oz

1. Preheat the grill until hot.
2. Generously spread four of the buttered bread slices with the pâté. Sprinkle with the herbs and salt and pepper to taste. Top with the mushrooms and then cover with the remaining bread slices to sandwich together.
3. Place on the grill rack and toast until golden on both sides, about 4–5 minutes. Turn over with tongs halfway through the cooking time.
4. Press down on the sandwiches firmly and cut each sandwich into two triangles. Serve at once.

Makes 4

Special Feature

Some Typical Garden Herbs

There are a great many herbs that can be used to flavour food and lots can be grown in the garden quite easily for use. The following basic herbs prove most versatile in cooking:

Parsley A mild, curly leaved herb that can be added freely to most dishes. Use in sprigs or chop with scissors to use.

Mint A fresh, sharp-pointed leaf herb that has a clean, minty smell and flavour. Use it with lamb, especially for mint sauce, potatoes and in chilled summer drinks.

Sage A strong, warm-flavoured herb that has an oval, broad, flat leaf. It is delicious with liver, pork and other rich meats.

Chives A herb with long thin spiky green stems that smells delicately of onion. It is usually scissor snipped and used in salads or eaten with cottage and cream cheese. Use it as a garnish over soups too.

Thyme A tiny leafed herb with a strong and penetrating flavour. Strip the leaves from the stem and use in stuffings and rice mixtures.

Rosemary A very distinctive herb with hard spiky green leaves and a beautiful blue flower. It is used with lamb, fish and chicken.

Chicken and Ham Stir-fried Rice

This is a speedy snack dish made using a stir-frying technique of cooking.

15 g	butter	$\frac{1}{2}$ oz
2	eggs, lightly beaten	2
4 tablespoons	oil	4 tablespoons
100 g	cooked ham, chopped	4 oz
450 g	cooked rice	1 lb
50 g	cooked chicken, chopped	2 oz
4	spring onions, chopped	4
100 g	beansprouts, washed	4 oz
	salt and pepper	
	chopped parsley to garnish	

1. Melt the butter in a frying pan. Add the eggs and cook for 2–3 minutes or until they are set on the underside. Stir the eggs with a fork and cook for a further 2–3 minutes. Transfer to a mixing bowl and break up with a fork.
2. Place the oil in a frying pan and heat until hot. Add the ham, rice, chicken and spring onions, blending well. Stir-fry over a high heat for 2 minutes – this means frying the food while stirring constantly.
3. Reduce the heat to low and add the beansprouts and chopped egg. Stir-fry for a further 2 minutes.
4. Add salt and pepper to taste and stir-fry for a further 1 minute or until the mixture is very hot.
5. Serve at once sprinkled with the chopped parsley.

Serves 4–6

Special Feature

To Sprout Beans

Beansprouts are useful ingredients to add to salads, Chinese-style stir-fried dishes and sandwich fillings. Almost any bean can be sprouted but the mung bean grows particularly quickly.

To sprout mung beans, wash the beans thoroughly. Place 2 tablespoons into a wide-necked jar and fill up with lukewarm water. Leave to stand overnight. Drain off the water, cover the jar with muslin and an elastic band, and leave the jar upside down to drain in a warm place. Every night and morning, until the sprouts are ready, rinse the beans in the jar with lukewarm water. Shake gently then drain thoroughly. Turn upside down again to drain. The sprouts will be ready in about 4 days by which time they will have grown to about 4–5 cm / 1$\frac{1}{2}$–2 inches in length.

FANTASTIC FAMILY FARE

Moussaka
(Illustrated opposite)

Moussaka is thought to be a Rumanian, Turkish or Greek dish and is just as popular in those countries as shepherd's pie is in Britain.

The aubergines must be dégorged before cooking (see page 40).

450 g	aubergines, sliced and dégorged	1 lb
3 tablespoons	oil	3 tablespoons
2	onions, peeled and sliced	2
450 g	minced lamb	1 lb
50 g	mushrooms, wiped and chopped	2 oz
1 (425-g) can	tomatoes	1 (15-oz) can
1 tablespoon	tomato purée	1 tablespoon
	salt and pepper	
	Topping	
2	eggs	2
150 ml	single cream or top of the milk	¼ pint
75 g	Cheddar cheese, grated	3 oz
	tomato wedges and parsley to garnish	

1. Preheat the oven to moderate (180°C, 350°F, Gas Mark 4).
2. Wash and dry the aubergine slices. Heat the oil in a large frying pan and fry the aubergine slices until golden, turning over once. Remove with a slotted spoon and drain on absorbent kitchen paper.
3. Add the onions to the pan juices and cook until softened, about 5 minutes.
4. Add the lamb and mushrooms, mixing well. Fry over a gentle heat for 10 minutes, stirring occasionally.
5. Add the tomatoes and their juice, tomato purée and salt and pepper to taste. Mix well to blend, bring to the boil, cover and simmer for 20 minutes.
6. Place a layer of aubergine slices in the bottom of a medium ovenproof dish. Top with a little lamb mixture. Continue to layer, finishing with a layer of the aubergines. Bake, uncovered, for 30 minutes.
7. To make the topping, beat the eggs with the cream or milk. Stir in the cheese and pour over the moussaka. Cook, uncovered, for a further 15–20 minutes until golden brown. Garnish with tomato wedges and a sprig of parsley and serve with a salad. **Serves 4**

Pear and Green Grape Salad
(Illustrated opposite)

This attractive salad dish is ideal to serve with cold roast meats left over from the Sunday joint. Use either Conference or Comice pears as liked. (Do you know the difference? See below.)

4	ripe pears	4
175 g	cream cheese	6 oz
3 tablespoons	mayonnaise	3 tablespoons
	salt and pepper	
	paprika pepper	
350 g	green grapes	12 oz
	lettuce leaves or watercress sprigs to garnish	

1. Halve the pears lengthways and peel carefully to remove the skin.
2. Remove the cores with a teaspoon and discard.
3. Place the cream cheese and mayonnaise in a bowl and mix well to blend. Add salt, pepper and paprika to taste.
4. Arrange the pear halves, cut side downwards, on a serving plate and coat with cheese mixture.
5. Halve and remove the seeds from the grapes and press on to the pears to cover them. Arrange the pears and grapes close together, if you like, so that they resemble a bunch of grapes.
6. Garnish with lettuce leaves or watercress sprigs.
Serves 4

Special Feature
A Juicy Pair

There are over 5,000 varieties of pear in existence, but two of the most popular are the Comice and Conference.

The Comice pear is the rounder shaped pear and is the sweeter and juicier of the two with a flesh that literally melts in the mouth.

The Conference pear is an excellent eating pear but also good for cooking and bottling. It is medium-sized, with an irregular, tapering shape. It can be eaten when firm and 'nutty' or can be ripened further at home.

Bottom, Sweet 'n' Sour Pork (page 36); *top*, Moussaka (opposite);
right, Pear and Green Grape Salad (opposite).

35

Sweet 'n' Sour Pork

(Illustrated on page 35)

Chinese take-aways have ensured that sweet 'n' sour pork is just as popular these days as fish and chips. Do take especial care when cooking with the hot oil.

900 g	lean pork, cut into 2-cm/¾-inch cubes	2 lb
2 teaspoons	salt	2 teaspoons
2 tablespoons	cornflour	2 tablespoons
8 tablespoons	self-raising flour	8 tablespoons
150 ml	water	¼ pint
2	eggs, beaten	2
	oil for deep frying	

Sauce

1 tablespoon	oil	1 tablespoon
1 large	green pepper, cored, seeded and sliced	1 large
1 large	red pepper, cored, seeded and sliced	1 large
1	onion, peeled and chopped	1
25 g	root ginger, peeled and very finely chopped	1 oz
3 tablespoons	cornflour	3 tablespoons
150 ml	water	¼ pint
6 tablespoons	wine vinegar	6 tablespoons
5 tablespoons	dark brown sugar	5 tablespoons
6 tablespoons	orange juice	6 tablespoons
4 tablespoons	dry ginger ale	4 tablespoons
3 tablespoons	soy sauce	3 tablespoons
4 tablespoons	tomato purée	4 tablespoons

1. Rub the pork with the salt and dust in the cornflour to coat on all sides.
2. Place the flour in a bowl and add the water and eggs. Whisk well to combine and make a batter.
3. Heat the oil in a large saucepan to 180°C/350°F or until hot. Coat the pieces of pork in the batter and add to the hot oil, taking special care not to splash the oil. Deep fry for about 5 minutes, or until golden brown. Remove with a slotted spoon and drain on absorbent kitchen paper.
4. Meanwhile, to make the sauce, heat the oil in a large frying pan until hot. Add the peppers, onion and root ginger. Stir-fry for 2 minutes.
5. Mix the cornflour with the water, wine vinegar, sugar, orange juice, ginger ale, soy sauce and tomato purée in a jug. Add to the vegetables and cook, stirring constantly until the mixture thickens and clears. Spoon over the cooked pork to serve.

Serves 4–6

Spaghetti and Sausagemeat Volcano

This is a clever and exciting way to serve sausagemeat 'rocks' on a potato and spaghetti 'volcano'.

450 g	pork sausagemeat	1 lb
1 tablespoon	flour	1 tablespoon
450 g	potatoes, peeled	1 lb
	salt	
50 g	butter	2 oz
	oil for frying	
1 (425-g) can	spaghetti in tomato sauce	1 (15-oz) can

1. Divide the sausagemeat into about 12 portions and shape each into a ball. Dust with the flour to coat.
2. Place the potatoes in a saucepan. Cover with water, add a little salt and bring to the boil. Lower the heat, cover and simmer for 20 minutes until soft. Drain through a colander and place in a mixing bowl.
3. Add the butter and mash, with a potato masher, until smooth.
4. Place a little oil in a frying pan and heat until hot. Add the sausagemeat balls and shallow fry for 6 minutes, turning to brown on all sides. Remove with a slotted spoon and drain on absorbent kitchen paper.
5. Meanwhile, open the can of spaghetti and place in a saucepan. Heat through until hot.
6. To serve, on a flat plate, make a 'mountain' of the mashed potato and hollow out the centre. Arrange the sausagemeat 'rocks' around the base. Spoon the spaghetti into the hollow and allow some to spill down the sides and on to the 'rocks'. **Serves 4**

Special Feature

Pasta is Easy to Cook

Pasta couldn't be simpler to cook. Canned pasta only needs to be heated through gently in a saucepan before eating. To cook dry pasta, just pop it into a large saucepan of boiling salted water for a few minutes and then drain. You could add a teaspoon of oil to the water to prevent the pasta from sticking together. Read the packet to see exactly how long the pasta needs to cook and time it yourself. The pasta should be what the Italians call 'al dente', which means that it is soft but still has a bite in it.

Now drain the pasta and it is ready to serve – top with a tomato or cheese sauce, use in a soup or salad or serve as a main meal accompaniment instead of rice or potatoes.

Savoury Mince with Crumble Thatch

(Illustrated on the frontispiece)

The basis for this main meal dish is a good savoury mince – it is endlessly versatile and can also be used for a bolognese sauce to serve with spaghetti or to layer between pasta for a lasagne.

	Savoury mince	
2 tablespoons	oil	2 tablespoons
1 rasher	bacon, rinded and chopped	1 rasher
1	onion, peeled and chopped	1
1	stick celery, scrubbed and chopped	1
1 large	carrot, peeled and chopped	1 large
450 g	lean minced beef	1 lb
1 (227-g) can	tomatoes, chopped	1 (8-oz) can
4 tablespoons	beef stock	4 tablespoons
	salt and pepper	
	Crumble thatch	
225 g	self-raising flour	8 oz
50 g	lard	2 oz
50 g	butter	2 oz
75 g	cheese, grated	3 oz
25 g	salted peanuts, chopped	1 oz

1. Preheat the oven to moderately hot (200°C, 400°F, Gas Mark 6).
2. Heat the oil in a large saucepan. Add the bacon, onion, celery and carrot, and fry over a moderate heat for 5 minutes.
3. Add the beef and cook for about 10 minutes until lightly browned.
4. Add the tomatoes, stock and salt and pepper to taste. Simmer over a gentle heat for about 15 minutes or until thick and bubbly. Spoon into an ovenproof dish.
5. Meanwhile, sift the flour with a pinch of salt into a bowl. Rub in the lard and butter with your fingertips until the mixture resembles fine breadcrumbs. Add the cheese and peanuts, mixing well to blend.
6. Spoon over the savoury mince mixture and level the surface with the back of a spoon. Bake in the oven for about 30 minutes, or until golden and cooked. Serve hot. **Serves 4–6**

Clapping Eggs

(Illustrated on the frontispiece)

On the Island of Anglesey, North Wales, on the Monday before Easter, a strange custom takes place – children are encouraged to go around clapping wooden boards and saying in Welsh 'clap, clap, an egg for the little boys of the parish'. This is a fertility rite to celebrate the oncoming of Easter and spring in general.

Clapping Eggs is a traditional Welsh dish that would prove suitable to serve on such a day but is good at any time of the year as a tasty and filling main meal. It is economical too since it does not contain any meat.

350 g	potatoes, peeled	12 oz
	salt and pepper	
6	leeks	6
40 g	butter	1½ oz
6	hard-boiled eggs, shelled	6
300 ml	hot cheese sauce (see page 13)	½ pint
25 g	cheese, grated	1 oz

1. Place the potatoes in a saucepan, cover with water, add a little salt and bring to the boil. Lower the heat, cover and simmer for 20 minutes until soft. Drain through a colander and place in a mixing bowl.
2. Meanwhile, trim and thoroughly wash the leeks under cold running water then cut into thin slices. Place in a saucepan with a little water, add a little salt and bring to the boil. Lower the heat, cover and simmer for 8–10 minutes until tender. Drain through a colander.
3. Add the butter and salt and pepper to taste to the potatoes and mash, with a potato masher, until smooth. Add the cooked leeks and mix well.
4. Preheat the grill to moderately hot.
5. Spoon the leek and potato mixture around the edge of a gratin or flameproof dish. Halve the eggs and place in the middle. Spoon the hot cheese sauce over the eggs to coat.
6. Sprinkle with the cheese and cook under the grill until golden and bubbly. Serve hot while still sizzling. **Serves 4**

Bottom, Orange Cheesecake (opposite); *on tray top left*, Jamaican Creams (page 41); *top right*, Tasty Lemon Ice Cream (opposite).

Orange Cheesecake
(Illustrated opposite)

This is a speedy cheesecake recipe using a jelly instead of powdered gelatine as the setting agent. Cut into wedges to serve.

	Base	
175 g	digestive biscuits	6 oz
40 g	butter	1½ oz
25 g	plain chocolate	1 oz
	Topping	
1 (312-g) can	mandarin oranges in syrup	1 (11-oz) can
3 tablespoons	water	3 tablespoons
1	orange jelly tablet	1
225 g	cream cheese	8 oz
150 ml	double cream	¼ pint

1. Lightly oil a 20-cm/8-inch loose-bottomed cake tin, using a pastry brush.
2. Place the biscuits in a plastic bag and crush with a rolling pin until they form fine crumbs.
3. Meanwhile, place the butter and chocolate in a bowl set over a saucepan of hot water. Stir until the butter and chocolate melt.
4. Add the biscuit crumbs to the chocolate mixture and stir well to blend. Spoon the mixture into the base of the tin, press down and level the surface with the back of a spoon. Leave in a cool place to become firm.
5. Drain the syrup from the mandarin oranges into a saucepan. Add the water and the broken up jelly tablet. Heat gently until the jelly dissolves.
6. Whisk in about a third of the mandarin oranges, lightly chopped, then chill until almost set.
7. Gradually whisk the setting jelly into the cream cheese, blending well.
8. Place the cream in a bowl and whip until it stands in soft peaks. Stir into the cream cheese mixture, blending well.
9. Spoon the filling over the base and chill until set, about 1 hour.
10. Decorate with the remaining mandarin oranges before serving.
11. To serve, push the base of the tin upwards, leaving the ring over your arm, and place the cheesecake on the work surface. Carefully remove from the base of the tin with a large spatula or metal fish slice and transfer to a serving plate.

Serves 8

Tasty Lemon Ice Cream
(Illustrated opposite)

This ice cream has a light creamy flavour and makes a super dessert to freeze away for later eating.

4	eggs, separated	4
300 ml	double cream	½ pint
250 ml	lemon curd (see page 58)	8 fl oz
50 g	icing sugar, sifted	2 oz
	fan wafers and lemon slices	

1. Place the egg yolks in a bowl. Whisk until very pale and thickened.
2. Gradually whisk in the cream and then the lemon curd until well blended.
3. Place the egg whites in a clean, grease-free bowl and whisk until they stand in stiff peaks. Add the sugar, a tablespoon at a time, and whisk until well blended.
4. Gently fold the lemon mixture into the egg whites with a metal spoon.
5. Transfer to a rigid polythene container, cover and freeze until firm, about 4–6 hours.
6. Serve scooped into dessert glasses and with fan wafers. Decorate with lemon slices, if liked.

Serves 6

Special Feature
Checking if Eggs are Fresh

When broken, a fresh egg smells pleasant, the yolk is round and firm and quite evenly distributed. A stale egg has a slight smell, and spreads out thinly when broken. A bad egg smells bad!

To test the freshness of an egg, place in a bowl of water—if it sinks it is fresh. If it rises slightly it is stale and if it floats or stands upright it is bad. This is because an egg shell is porous, so if an egg is stored for a long time, some of the water content will evaporate and the airspace at the rounded end of the egg will enlarge, enabling it to float.

Speedy Pizza
(Illustrated on back cover)

A pizza is an Italian speciality consisting of bread dough, shaped into a round and covered with a tomato topping, cheese and other savoury ingredients. The bread dough base can be a little complicated to make and takes a long time to prepare – but the recipe below gives a speedy recipe for pizza using a very simple scone pastry dough which can be made in minutes.

	Base	
100 g	self-raising flour	4 oz
½ teaspoon	baking powder	½ teaspoon
½ teaspoon	salt	½ teaspoon
15 g	butter	½ oz
5 tablespoons	milk	5 tablespoons
	Filling	
1 (425-g) can	tomatoes, drained	1 (15-oz) can
1 small	onion, peeled and chopped	1 small
1 tablespoon	tomato purée	1 tablespoon
1 teaspoon	dried mixed herbs	1 teaspoon
	salt and pepper	
	Topping	
75 g	Cheddar or Mozzarella cheese, sliced	3 oz
50 g	spicy delicatessen sausage, sliced (optional)	2 oz
	olives	
	chopped parsley	

1. Preheat the oven to moderately hot (200°C, 400°F, Gas Mark 6).
2. Sift the flour, baking powder and salt into a bowl. Rub in the butter with your fingertips until the mixture resembles fine breadcrumbs. Add the milk and mix with a fork to a soft dough.
3. Using a floured rolling pin, roll out the pastry on a lightly floured surface to a round about 20 cm/8 inches in diameter. Place on a greased baking tray.
4. Meanwhile, chop the tomatoes coarsely with a knife and place in a saucepan. Add the onion, tomato purée and herbs and stir well to mix. Cook uncovered over a moderate heat for about 15–20 minutes, stirring occasionally, until the mixture is thick and pulpy. Add salt and pepper to taste.
5. Spoon over the pizza base to within 2.5 cm/1 inch of the edge.
6. Arrange the cheese, sausage (if used) and olives on top of the pizza.
7. Bake for about 30 minutes or until well risen and golden brown.
8. Sprinkle with chopped parsley and serve hot or cold cut into wedges. **Serves 4**

One Pan Sausage Supper
(Illustrated on frontispiece)

Everyone seems to like cooking and eating but few people enjoy the washing up. Reduce it to the very minimum by cooking a complete meal in just one pan!

15 g	lard	½ oz
450 g	pork sausages	1 lb
1	onion, peeled and sliced	1
½	green pepper, cored, seeded and sliced	½
1 small	aubergine, sliced and dégorged (see below)	1 small
2	courgettes, sliced	2
4	tomatoes, sliced	4
	salt and pepper	
300 ml	light chicken stock	½ pint
	Dumplings	
100 g	self-raising flour	4 oz
50 g	shredded suet	2 oz
¼ teaspoon	salt	¼ teaspoon
½ teaspoon	mustard powder	½ teaspoon
5 tablespoons	water	5 tablespoons

1. Place the lard in a large deep frying pan or wide-based shallow saucepan and heat until hot.
2. Add the sausages and quickly fry on all sides until brown.
3. Add the onion, pepper, aubergine, courgettes and tomatoes and fry for 1 minute. Add salt and pepper.
4. Add the stock, blending well, and bring to the boil.
5. Meanwhile, mix the flour with the suet, salt and mustard powder. Add the water and bind together, with a fork, to make a firm dough. Divide into eight portions and roll each into a ball.
6. Add to the sausage mixture, cover and cook over a gentle simmering heat for 20 minutes. Serve hot.

Serves 4

Special Feature

Dégorging Aubergines

Dégorging is a term used in French cooking which generally means to soak a food in cold water to remove a strong bitter flavour, or to remove excess water prior to cooking in the case of aubergines and cucumber.

To dégorge, thinly slice the vegetable, sprinkle with salt and place in a colander. Leave to drain for about 1 hour. Rinse with cold water then pat dry with kitchen paper.

Jamaican Creams
(Illustrated on page 38)

Did you know that 4,000 coffee beans – one tree's average annual harvest – are needed to produce 450 g/1 lb ground coffee? Fortunately it only takes four hungry people to eat this delicious dessert made with custard, bananas and instant coffee.

40 g	custard powder	1½ oz
40 g	sugar	1½ oz
450 ml	milk	¾ pint
2	bananas	2
1 teaspoon	instant coffee powder	1 teaspoon
150 ml	double cream	¼ pint
	grated chocolate to sprinkle	

1. Mix the custard powder, sugar and a little of the milk together in a mixing bowl. Place the remaining milk in a saucepan and bring to the boil. Carefully pour over the custard powder mixture and beat very well to combine.
2. Return the custard to the saucepan and bring to the boil, stirring all the time until thick and smooth. Pour into a bowl, cover with cling film to prevent a skin forming and leave to cool.
3. Meanwhile, purée the bananas in a blender or mash until smooth then pass through a fine nylon sieve.
4. Stir the coffee and banana purée into the cool custard, blending well.
5. Whip the cream until it stands in soft peaks. Fold half the cream into the custard mixture with a metal spoon. Carefully spoon into four dessert glasses. Top with the remaining cream – it looks very attractive if swirled with a teaspoon, or you could place the mixture in a piping bag fitted with a star-shaped nozzle and pipe swirls on top of the dessert. Sprinkle with grated chocolate.
6. Chill for 1–2 hours until very cold before serving.

Serves 4

Banana and Walnut Loaf
(Illustrated on page 43)

This cake could be called a 'cut-and-come-again loaf' since it keeps beautifully moist over several days if kept in an airtight tin. Eat it plain or spread with butter.

100 g	butter or margarine	4 oz
175 g	light muscovado sugar	6 oz
2	ripe bananas, peeled and mashed	2
2	eggs, beaten	2
225 g	self-raising flour	8 oz
1 teaspoon	baking powder	1 teaspoon
50 g	walnuts, chopped	2 oz
2 tablespoons	milk	2 tablespoons

1. Preheat the oven to moderate (180°C, 350°F, Gas Mark 4). Grease and line a 1-kg/2-lb loaf tin (see below).
2. Place the butter or margarine and sugar in a mixing bowl and cream with a wooden spoon until light and fluffy.
3. Add the bananas and eggs and beat well to mix thoroughly.
4. Sift the flour with the baking powder and fold into the banana mixture with a metal spoon until well combined.
5. Add the walnuts and milk and stir gently to mix. Spoon into the prepared tin and level the surface.
6. Bake for about 1 hour until the loaf is well-risen, golden brown and firm to the touch.
7. Turn out and leave to cool on a wire rack.

Makes 1 (1-kg/2-lb) loaf

Special Feature

Lining Cake Tins

Lining a Sandwich Tin Lightly grease the inside of the tin with a little butter or brush with oil. Cut out a circle of greaseproof paper to fit the base of the tin (this is best done by standing the tin on a sheet of paper, drawing around it with a pencil and then cutting out). Line the tin with the greaseproof circle and grease again.

Lining a Deep Cake or Loaf Tin Cut a strip of greaseproof paper to fit the sides of the tin – about 5 cm/2 inches wider than the depth. Make a 2.5-cm/1-inch fold along the length of the strip, cutting this fold at 1-cm/½-inch intervals, at an angle. Place this strip of greaseproof paper around the inside of the greased tin, with the snipped fold lying flat against the base. Cut a circle, square or oblong to fit the base of the tin as above and place in the base. Brush the base and sides again with oil or melted fat.

Chocolate Brownies
(Illustrated opposite)

Brownies are moist, sticky squares of chocolate cake made with walnuts and, in this case, raisins. They originate from America where they are a popular lunch box item but are also served with whipped cream as a family dessert.

100 g	butter	4 oz
100 g	plain chocolate	4 oz
100 g	soft brown sugar	4 oz
100 g	self-raising flour	4 oz
	pinch of salt	
2	eggs, beaten	2
50 g	walnuts, chopped	2 oz
25 g	raisins	1 oz
1–2 tablespoons	milk	1–2 tablespoons
	icing sugar to sift	

1. Preheat the oven to moderate (180°C, 350°F, Gas Mark 4). Grease a 20-cm/8-inch square cake tin.
2. Place the butter and chocolate in a bowl set over a saucepan of hot water. Stir until the chocolate and butter melt. Remove from the heat, stir in the sugar and leave to cool.
3. Sift the flour and salt into a bowl. Make a well in the centre and pour in the chocolate mixture. Add the eggs and beat well with a wooden spoon to blend.
4. Add the walnuts, raisins and enough milk to make a mixture with a soft dropping consistency.
5. Pour into the prepared tin and bake for about 30 minutes or until a skewer inserted into the centre of the cake comes out clean of mixture.
6. Leave to cool in the tin for about 10 minutes. Turn out on to a wire rack to cool. Cut into squares when cold and sift over a little icing sugar.

Makes 16 squares

Variations

Pecan Chocolate Brownies Prepare and cook as above but use 75 g/3 oz chopped pecans instead of the walnuts and raisins.

Chocolate and Ginger Brownies Prepare and cook as above but use 25 g/1 oz chopped crystallised ginger instead of the raisins.

Coconut Lemon Cheese Flan
(Illustrated opposite)

This is a refrigerator dessert that is also delicious for tea-time eating.

275 g	coconut cookie biscuits	10 oz
125 g	butter	4½ oz
1	lemon jelly tablet	1
	juice of 2 lemons	
225 g	cream cheese	8 oz
1 (44-g) sachet	dessert topping mix	1 (1½-oz) sachet
150 ml	cold milk	¼ pint
	lemon slices and whipped cream	

1. Lightly grease a 23-cm/9-inch flan dish.
2. Place the biscuits in a plastic bag and crush with a rolling pin until they form fine crumbs.
3. Meanwhile, melt the butter in a saucepan.
4. Add the butter to the biscuit crumbs and stir well to blend. Spoon the mixture into the flan dish and use to coat the sides and base evenly. Leave in a cool place to become firm.
5. Break up the jelly tablet and place the cubes in a bowl. Add 300 ml/½ pint boiling water and stir until the jelly dissolves. Add the lemon juice and cool.
6. When cold, whisk in the cream cheese.
7. Make up the dessert topping using the milk. Whisk into the lemon mixture, blending well.
8. Pour over the biscuit base and chill until set.
9. Decorate with lemon slices and whipped cream.

Serves 6–8

Special Feature

Citrus Fruit Garnishes

Slices of lemon, orange, grapefruit and lime make super garnishes for sweet and savoury dishes.

Citrus Twists Cut the fruit into thin slices. Using a serrated knife, cut each slice once from the edge to the centre. Open the cut and twist each slice in opposite directions to make a twist that will stand.

Citrus Cartwheels Using a special paring knife, thinly pare the rind along the length of the fruit at regular intervals. Thinly slice the fruit crossways to make notched slices that resemble cartwheels.

Citrus Butterflies Cut the fruit into thin slices and then again into half moons. Using a serrated knife, cut again from the outside peel edge almost into the centre. Open out to form butterfly wings.

Top left, Banana and Walnut Loaf (page 41); *top right*, Chocolate Brownies (opposite);
bottom, Coconut Lemon Cheese Flan (opposite).

Special Occasion Cookery

Cheddar Sails
(Illustrated on the back cover)

Cheddar sails are tempting party sandwiches made using French bread. The sails are edible cheese slices safely secured to the boat with cocktail sticks.

75 g	Cheddar cheese, grated	3 oz
1 large	carrot, peeled and grated	1 large
3 tablespoons	salad cream	3 tablespoons
	salt and pepper	
8	slices French bread	8
8	slices tomato or cucumber	8
2	slices processed cheese	2
8	cocktail sticks	8
	shredded lettuce to serve	

1. Place the grated cheese, carrot, salad cream and salt and pepper to taste in a bowl. Mix well to blend.
2. Evenly spread the cheese and carrot mixture on to each slice of French bread.
3. Top each slice of bread with a tomato or cucumber slice.
4. Cut each cheese slice into four triangles.
5. Thread each cheese triangle on to a cocktail stick to make a sail and use to secure each tomato or cucumber slice on to the bread.
6. Line a large plate or board with shredded lettuce. Set the boats asail on top to serve. **Makes 8.**

Variations

Ham Sails Prepare as above but use 2 slices shoulder ham instead of the slices of processed cheese. Cut each slice of ham into four triangles.

Cheesy Sails Prepare as above but use 8 small pre-packed triangles of soft cream cheese or individual portions of processed cheese instead of the slices of processed cheese.

Chicken Sails Prepare as above but use four slices of cooked chicken roll instead of the slices of processed cheese. Cut each slice in half and thread each half onto a cocktail stick to make a "double" sail.

Spinning Catherine Wheel Sandwich Board

It is interesting to arrange sandwiches to form a centre-piece for a tea time or birthday party. This sandwich board is made of dainty pinwheel sandwiches with a tomato rosette centre.

25 g	butter	1 oz
3 tablespoons	mayonnaise	3 tablespoons
2 small	hard-boiled eggs, shelled and finely chopped	2 small
25 g	cream cheese	1 oz
40 g	Cheddar cheese, grated	1½ oz
2 tablespoons	snipped chives	2 tablespoons
	salt and pepper	
1	stick celery, scrubbed	1
4	slices brown bread, crusts removed	4
1 large	tomato	1 large

1. Place the butter and mayonnaise in a bowl and beat until smooth. Divide the mixture in half and stir the chopped eggs into one portion, blending well. Add the cream cheese, Cheddar cheese and chives to the second portion, blending well. Season both with salt and pepper to taste.
2. Cut the celery lengthways into four pieces, the same length as the bread slices.
3. Roll out the bread lightly with a rolling pin and spread half with the egg filling and half with the cheese filling.
4. Place a piece of celery across one end of each slice. Roll up, pressing the seam edge down lightly, to give a Swiss Roll effect.
5. Using a serrated knife, cut the rolls into 1-cm/½-inch slices to make pinwheels.
6. To make a tomato rosette, using a sharp serrated knife, start at the smooth end of the tomato and carefully cut away the skin in one continuous strip. Roll up the skin to form a rose and secure with half a cocktail stick.
7. To assemble the pinwheel, place the rose in the centre of a serving plate or board and surround with overlapping circles of the pinwheel sandwiches, allowing the last few to trail off straight like a spinning catherine wheel. Cover with cling film and chill until required. **Serves 2–4**

Chocolate Moon Rocket

This is one of the simplest birthday cakes to make – it uses one large ready-made chocolate Swiss roll, three mini chocolate rolls and two small sponge squares for its structure!

175 g	butter	6 oz
350 g	icing sugar	12 oz
175 g	plain chocolate, melted	6 oz
2	chocolate-flavoured mini sponge squares (Triple Deckers, for example)	2
1	chocolate-flavoured large Swiss roll	1
3	chocolate-flavoured mini Swiss rolls	3
	red dragées or red sugar strands to decorate	
1	ice cream wafer cone	1
	silver dragées to decorate	
	coloured glacé icing or novelties to decorate	

1 Place the butter in a bowl and beat with a wooden spoon until softened.
2 Gradually add the icing sugar and beat until fluffy. Add the melted chocolate and mix well to blend.
3 Place the sponge squares side by side on a cake board or serving plate and coat with about one-third of the chocolate icing.
4 Position the large Swiss roll in an upright position on top of the sponge squares. Coat the sides and top of the roll with about one-third of the chocolate icing.
5 Carefully coat about one-half of each of the mini rolls in the remaining icing and dip in red dragées or sugar strands. Position, at an angle, around the base of the 'rocket' to represent the firing jets of the rocket.
6 Carefully coat the ice cream cone with the remaining icing. Dip the pointed end in a few silver dragées and position on top of the sponge roll to represent the nose of the rocket.
7 Decorate the base and sides of the rocket with coloured glacé icing or try novelties if liked. Ideas include a rocket name, base name and toy astronauts. **Serves 10–12**

Honey and Chocolate Yule Log

This is a really festive yule log that is made with honey, eggs and wholemeal flour instead of the traditional Swiss roll mixture. Decorate with holly, fir cones, robins or other Christmas novelties for a stunning tea time centrepiece.

	Cake	
3	eggs	3
75 g	set or creamed honey	3 oz
75 g	plain wholemeal flour	3 oz
	Filling	
40 g	nibbed almonds, toasted	1½ oz
150 ml	double cream, whipped	¼ pint
	Covering	
225 g	plain chocolate	8 oz
50 g	butter	2 oz
	icing sugar to dust	

1 Preheat the oven to moderately hot (200°C, 400°F, Gas Mark 6). Grease and line a 33 × 23-cm / 13 × 9-inch Swiss roll tin with greaseproof paper. Grease the lining paper.
2 Place the eggs and honey in a bowl and stand over a saucepan of hot water. Whisk until the mixture is thick and pale. It should be thick enough to leave a distinctive trail when you lift the whisk. Remove from the heat and continue whisking until cool.
3 Carefully fold the flour into the mixture using a metal spoon. When evenly mixed, turn the mixture into the lined tin, spreading it over the whole of the base.
4 Bake for about 10 minutes until golden and firm to the touch.
5 Meanwhile, place a clean damp tea towel on to the worktop and cover this with a sheet of greaseproof paper. Sprinkle with a little caster sugar. When the roll is cooked, quickly turn it out on to the sugared paper and peel off the lining paper. Trim the crusty edges from the cake with a sharp knife. Using the tea towel as a guide, roll up the sponge from the short end with the greaseproof paper inside.
6 When completely cool, unroll the sponge. Fold the almonds into the whipped cream and spread over the sponge. Roll up again and place on a wire rack.
7 Place the chocolate and butter in a saucepan and heat *very* gently to melt. Spread over the yule log with a palette knife to coat. Swirl the chocolate icing into notches like the bark of a tree. Leave to set.
8 When set, dust with a little icing sugar. Place on a serving plate and decorate further as liked.
Serves 6

Cheesy Party Nibbles
(Illustrated opposite)

This quick and easy recipe for cheesy nibbles takes no time to make – a good thing too since they will disappear just as quickly at any party celebration.

100 g	plain flour	4 oz
1 teaspoon	mustard powder	1 teaspoon
	salt and pepper	
100 g	butter	4 oz
100 g	Cheddar cheese, grated	4 oz
	beaten egg to glaze	
	chopped nuts or seeds to garnish (peanuts, sesame seeds or poppy seeds, for example)	

1. Preheat the oven to moderately hot (200°C, 400°F, Gas Mark 6). Lightly grease two baking trays.
2. Sift the flour, mustard powder and a little salt and pepper into a bowl.
3. Rub in the butter with your fingertips until the mixture resembles fine breadcrumbs.
4. Add the cheese and mix very well with a fork and then your hands to make a firm dough.
5. Roll out on a lightly floured surface using a floured rolling pin to about 5 mm/¼ inch thickness. Stamp out or cut out small shapes as liked. For example, if the nibbles are being made for a Christmas party cut out stars, Christmas trees, bells or snowmen.
6. Place on the prepared baking trays, brush to glaze with beaten egg and sprinkle with chopped nuts or seeds.
7. Bake for 10–15 minutes or until golden. Allow to cool on the trays. Store in an airtight tin until required.
8. If liked the biscuits can be piped or spread with cream cheese or pâté for serving. **Makes 20–30**

Mothering Sunday Nest
(Illustrated opposite)

It is traditional to serve simnel cake on Mothering Sunday – a rich fruit cake that is topped with almond paste shaped into 11 small eggs. Some say that the 11 eggs represent the disciples around the table at the Last Supper, while others say they represent the 11 months that young working girls were often away from their mothers – they were only allowed home for the twelfth month of the year to celebrate Mothering Sunday.

Simnel cake is a little difficult to make but this nest with its speckled eggs is very easy.

1	large sponge flan case (bought)	1
Filling		
225 g	plain chocolate	8 oz
4 tablespoons	water	4 tablespoons
100 g	butter	4 oz
100 g	caster sugar	4 oz
1 (440-g) can	sweetened chestnut purée	1 (15½-oz) can
2 tablespoons	orange cordial	2 tablespoons
Nest		
50 g	butter	2 oz
2 tablespoons	golden syrup	2 tablespoons
25 g	cocoa powder	1 oz
50 g	caster sugar	2 oz
50 g	crispy rice cereal	2 oz
Speckled eggs		
150 g	marzipan	5 oz
2 teaspoons	grated chocolate	2 teaspoons

1. For the filling, place the chocolate and water in a saucepan and heat gently until melted. Allow to cool.
2. Cream the butter and sugar together until light and fluffy. Gradually add the chestnut purée, beating well. Stir in the melted chocolate mixture and orange cordial. Spoon into the flan case and chill in the refrigerator until firm.
3. Make the nest by melting the butter and syrup in a saucepan. Remove from the heat and stir in the cocoa powder. Add the sugar and cereal and toss gently to coat. Spoon evenly around the top edge of the flan to make a nest.
4. Knead the marzipan and chocolate together, taking care not to overmix so that the mixture still has a speckled appearance. Divide into 11 pieces and mould each into an egg shape. Place the eggs evenly over the flan.
5. Decorate with a large coloured ribbon bow at the side of the flan if liked. Cut into wedges to serve. **Serves 10–12**

Centre, Sausage Wrappers (page 48); *top*, Mothering Sunday Nest (opposite) and Coloured Easter Eggs (page 48); *bottom*, Cheesy Party Nibbles (opposite).

Sponge Igloo

This is a delicious pudding to serve at a special occasion meal. Inside the golden baked meringue crust is enticingly cool ice cream – choose your own favourite flavour.

1 small	round Victoria sandwich cake (see page 17)	1 small
1 (1-litre) block	ice cream (flavour as liked)	1 (35.2-fl oz) block
	Topping	
3	egg whites	3
150 g	caster sugar	5 oz

1. Preheat the oven to hot (230°C, 450°F, Gas Mark 8).
2. Place the cake on a shallow ovenproof plate. Place the ice cream brick on top of the cake so that it fits neatly. Keep cool in the refrigerator or freezer.
3. Meanwhile, place the egg whites in a clean bowl and whisk until they stand in stiff peaks. Gradually add half the sugar, a tablespoon at a time, and whisk until very thick and glossy. Fold in the remaining sugar with a metal spoon.
4. Spoon the meringue over the ice cream and cake to completely cover. Use a palette knife to swirl.
5. Bake in the oven for 3–5 minutes or until the meringue is tinged golden. Serve at once.

Serves 8

Coloured Easter Eggs
(Illustrated on page 47)

Decorated eggs are firm family favourites to eat at Easter time. It is easy to make coloured eggs for eating if you follow the instructions below – but remember for each colour you choose you will need a separate saucepan for cooking.

eggs
vinegar
vegetable food colourings
felt-tip pens or paints to decorate

1. Place the number of eggs to be coloured and decorated in a bowl. Cover with vinegar, leave to stand for 30 minutes and then drain.
2. Place in a saucepan with water to cover and the food colouring of your choice. Soft-boil for 4 minutes or cook for 10 minutes to hard-boil.
3. Remove with a slotted spoon. Place soft-boiled eggs in egg cups and very quickly decorate with felt-tip pens. Serve at once.
4. Plunge hard-boiled eggs into cold water and leave until cold. Dry, then decorate.

Sausage Wrappers
(Illustrated on page 47)

Sausage wrappers are just the food to serve on November 5th's Bonfire Night or Halloween (October 31st) alongside sweet treats like bonfire toffee, toffee apples and parkin or gingerbread.

8	thin slices white bread	8
2 tablespoons	tomato ketchup	2 tablespoons
8	pork chipolata sausages, cooked	8
4	rashers streaky bacon, rinded	4
15 g	butter, melted	½ oz

1. Preheat the oven to moderately hot (200°C, 400°F, Gas Mark 6).
2. Using a sharp knife, remove the crusts from the bread. Spread each slice of bread with the tomato ketchup.
3. Place a sausage on each slice of bread and roll up to enclose.
4. Place the bacon rashers on a board and stretch with the back of a knife then cut in half.
5. Roll each piece of bacon around the centre of the rolls. Place on a baking tray and brush the bread still visible with melted butter.
6. Bake for 10–15 minutes until the bacon is cooked and the bread is golden brown. Serve with paper napkins to hold. **Makes 8**

Hot Air Balloon Cake

(Illustrated on the back cover)

This is a very colourful and impressive birthday party cake that looks far more difficult to prepare than it really is. The secret is to bake one of the cakes in a ring mould. Fill the centre of the cake with colourful sweets and write the name of the birthday girl or boy on the balloon.

	Cake	
250 g	plain flour	9 oz
3 tablespoons	cocoa powder	3 tablespoons
1½ teaspoons	bicarbonate of soda	1½ teaspoons
1½ teaspoons	baking powder	1½ teaspoons
210 g	caster sugar	7½ oz
3 tablespoons	golden syrup	3 tablespoons
3 large	eggs	3 large
225 ml	corn oil	8 fl oz
225 ml	milk	8 fl oz
	Chocolate icing	
175 g	butter	6 oz
350 g	icing sugar	12 oz
175 g	plain chocolate, melted	6 oz
	Decoration	
4	long coloured straws	4
1	round balloon	1
	felt-tip pens or paints	
	coloured ribbon	
	small colourful sweets	
	marzipan or novelty people or animals	

1. Preheat the oven to moderate (160°C, 325°F, Gas Mark 3).
2. Grease and line two 20-cm/8-inch shallow sandwich tins. Grease and base-line a 20-cm/8-inch diameter ring mould.
3. Sift the flour, cocoa powder, bicarbonate of soda and baking powder into a bowl. Add the sugar and stir well together.
4. Mix the golden syrup with the eggs, corn oil and milk. Whisk into the flour mixture until very well blended.
5. Divide evenly between the sandwich tins and ring mould. Bake in the oven for 30–40 minutes or until the cakes spring back when touched lightly with the fingertips. Turn out carefully on to a wire rack to cool.
6. Meanwhile, prepare the icing. Place the butter in a bowl and beat with a wooden spoon until softened. Gradually add the icing sugar and beat until fluffy. Add the melted chocolate and mix well to blend.
7. Sandwich the two layer cakes together with a little of the icing and place on a cake board or serving plate. Spread over a little more icing and top with the chocolate ring cake to make the balloon basket.
8. Place the remaining icing in a piping bag fitted with a star nozzle and pipe around the whole of the basket in small swirls to coat completely. Alternatively, and for a more professional look, divide the icing and place half in a piping bag fitted with a plain writing nozzle, and half in a piping bag fitted with a basket weave nozzle.
9. To begin the basket weave effect, pipe a vertical line down the cake using the writing nozzle. Pipe small short horizontal lines across the vertical line, in even spaces, using the basket weave nozzle. Continue piping with vertical lines and more horizontal weaving to go completely around and cover the cake.
10. Stick the four straws evenly into the cake at the four 'corners' to anchor the balloon. Use a fine skewer to make a neat hole if necessary. Bring the straws up to meet over the centre of the cake and fasten the ends together with a little sellotape.
11. Paint or write a message or name on the balloon with felt-tip pens or paints. Attach to the straws by the tie-end with a little more sellotape then tie a bow with the ribbon and leave to trail.
12. Fill the centre of the basket with sweets and marzipan or novelty people or animals.

Serves up to 20

Special Feature

Making a Paper Icing Bag

1. Cut out a 25-cm/10-inch square of greaseproof paper. Fold in half diagonally forming a triangle.
2. Roll corner B so that it lies inside corner A.
3. Bring corner C round so that the outside of the bag lies behind corner A.
4. Carefully shuffle the paper so that all three corners are together and the base forms into a sharp neat point.
5. Staple or fold the three points together to secure tightly.
6. Cut off the top of the bag with scissors. Drop the piping nozzle into the bag and ease into position. Spoon in the icing to use.

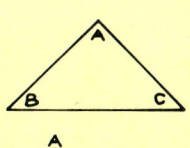

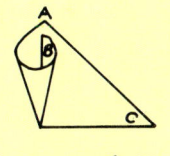

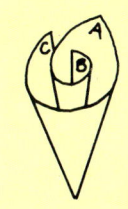

OUTDOOR FOOD AND FOOD FOR FREE

American Hamburgers
(Illustrated opposite)

A favourite and traditional American food, hamburgers can be grilled in the kitchen or cooked over an outdoor barbecue. Serve in true American style with a selection of pickles and relishes, tomato ketchup, mayonnaise, mustard, potato crisps, chips or French fries and, to drink, a fizzy cola.

675 g	lean minced beef	1½ lb
25 g	fresh breadcrumbs	1 oz
½ teaspoon	salt	½ teaspoon
¼ teaspoon	black pepper	¼ teaspoon
¼ teaspoon	dried thyme	¼ teaspoon
1 small	egg, lightly beaten	1 small
To Serve		
4	hamburger or large soft buns	4
40 g	butter	1½ oz
4	lettuce leaves	4
2 small	tomatoes, thinly sliced	2 small
1 small	onion, peeled and sliced into rings	1 small

1. Preheat the grill to hot or prepare a barbecue with medium coals.
2. Place the beef, breadcrumbs, salt, pepper, thyme and egg in a bowl. Mix with your hands to blend thoroughly. Divide the mixture into four portions and shape each into a ball, then flatten into patty or hamburger shapes and set aside.
3. Split the hamburger buns in half using a bread knife and butter each half.
4. Place the hamburgers on the grill rack and cook for 2–3 minutes on each side or until well browned. Reduce the heat to low and cook for a further 2–3 minutes on each side or until the hamburgers are adequately cooked. Alternatively cook the hamburgers on the barbecue for about 5–6 minutes on each side.
5. Place a lettuce leaf on the base of each bun half. Top with a hamburger, a few slices of tomato, a few onion rings and the bun lid. Serve at once with any accompaniments. **Serves 4**

Special Feature

Impromptu Barbecues

A barbecue is really little more than a grill on which food can be cooked over a fire-bed of glowing hot coals. Very simple forms of this arrangement can be improvised with a grill pan rack or a double thickness of chicken wire on a large flower pot, an old grill rack placed on top of a sturdy metal biscuit tin punctured with holes, or a chicken wire frame over loose bricks. An old metal wheelbarrow can also be used as a barbecue base.

It is a great outdoor party idea to rig up a range of clay pot barbecues to cook a variety of food from hamburgers to fruit kebabs.

To make the flower pot barbecues, line the inside of each 23-cm/9-inch deep clay flower pot with foil. Fill about one-third full with sand. Add a fire-lighter and about eight compressed charcoal briquettes. Stand the pot on four bricks or place in a clay saucer. Light and leave to burn for 30 minutes or until the briquettes glow red by night or have a fine grey ash by day. Top each flowerpot with a metal cooking rack or chicken wire frame, or place food on long skewers that fit across the top.

Raspberry Yogurt Jellies
(Illustrated on page 54)

These are delicious fruit-filled creamy jellies that are set in individual pots. Simply cover with cling film to take for a packed meal dessert. You can vary this recipe by changing the jelly or yogurt flavour.

1	raspberry jelly tablet	1
300 ml	boiling water	½ pint
100 g	frozen raspberries	4 oz
2 (150-g) cartons	raspberry yogurt	2 (5.3-oz) cartons

1. Divide the jelly into cubes and place in a large measuring jug. Add the boiling water and stir until the jelly dissolves. Allow to cool slightly.
2. Add the frozen raspberries and yogurt and mix well to blend.
3. Pour into five individual pots and chill until set. **Makes 5**

Bottom, American Hamburgers (opposite); *top*, Green Tomato Chutney (page 52); *right*, Apple and Leek Soup (page 52).

Green Tomato Chutney
(Illustrated on page 51)

In the late summer months almost anyone will give you the remaining green tomatoes from their crop since it is very unlikely they will ripen further in the sun or even indoors. Use them to make a super chutney for eating with hamburgers, grills and sandwiches throughout the winter.

900 g	green tomatoes, chopped	2 lb
1	red pepper, cored, seeded and chopped	1
1	green pepper, cored, seeded and chopped	1
1 large	onion, peeled and chopped	1 large
225 ml	distilled white vinegar	8 fl oz
250 g	caster sugar	9 oz
1 teaspoon	curry powder	1 teaspoon
1 tablespoon	mustard powder	1 tablespoon
1 teaspoon	ground ginger	1 teaspoon
	pinch of ground cloves, allspice, cinnamon and chilli powder	
$\frac{1}{2}$ teaspoon	ground black pepper	$\frac{1}{2}$ teaspoon

1. Place the tomatoes, peppers, onion and vinegar in a bowl, mixing well. Cover and leave to stand overnight.
2. Transfer to a large pan. Add the sugar and heat until the sugar dissolves. Add the curry powder, mustard powder, ginger, cloves, allspice, cinnamon and chilli powder. Mix well to blend. Bring to the boil, lower the heat and simmer for 10 minutes.
3. Pour into warmed preserving jars, cover with glass discs fitted with rubber rings and screw bands or clips, or seal with vinegar-proof preserving paper while still hot. Label and store.

Makes 1.5 kg/3 lb

Special Feature

Spicing Food Up

Undoubtedly a pinch or two of some spices can liven up a typical dish. But do you know your spices? Here are just a few:

Chilli Powder A hot, pungent pepper-based spice.
Cloves A spice with a warm sweet flavour, ideal to use with ham and in pickles.
Cinnamon A spice with a distinctive sweet spicy flavour, splendid to use with apples. Available ground or in long sticks.
Ginger A spice with a hot rich flavour used in making gingerbreads, ginger beer and other ginger desserts.
Nutmeg A spice with an exotic sweet spicy flavour. Use to sprinkle over baked custard tarts or rice puddings.

Apple and Leek Soup
(Illustrated on page 51)

This is a marvellous warming soup to serve outdoors, for a summer barbecue or an autumn bonfire party.

450 g	leeks, washed	1 lb
450 g	apples, dessert or cooking (see below)	1 lb
225 g	potatoes	8 oz
1	parsnip	1
50 g	butter	2 oz
600 ml	chicken stock	1 pint
1 teaspoon	chopped mixed herbs	1 teaspoon
	salt and pepper	
150 ml	single cream	$\frac{1}{4}$ pint
	chopped parsley or watercress to garnish	

1. Slice the leeks thinly on a wooden board. Peel, core and slice the apples. Peel and chop the potatoes and parsnip.
2. Melt the butter in a large saucepan. Add the leeks, apples, potatoes and parsnip and stir well to coat in the butter. Cook over a gentle heat until softened, about 10 minutes. Keep the lid on the pan and stir frequently.
3. Add the stock, herbs and salt and pepper. Cover and simmer for 1 hour, until the potatoes are soft.
4. Purée in a blender or pass through a fine sieve into a bowl. Return to the pan and stir in the cream, blending well. Reheat gently but do not boil.
5. Pour into mugs and sprinkle with a little parsley.

Serves 4–6

Special Feature

Polish Up Your English

Discovery A much sought after new dessert apple. It has a bright red skin with yellow streaks. It is firm and juicy and keeps well. In season from August to September.
Cox's Orange Pippin The finest flavoured of all dessert apples. The colour of Cox is variable – usually palish green with orange to red finish. In season from late September to May.
Bramley's Seedling The best known British cooking apple, ideal for stewing and baking. It has a deep green waxy skin. Available virtually all year round.
Worcester Pearmain A rich red apple with some pale green streaks, it is very juicy and sweet. In season September to November.
Egremont Russet An easy to recognise apple with a russet-brown skin and orange blush. It is crisp with a nutty flavour and in season from late September to January.

Picnic Sandwich Box

This is literally a bloomer loaf baked with its filling and cut into thick slices to serve. A 'bloomer' loaf is a long baton-shaped loaf with a series of diagonal slashes across the top; it is also sometimes called a twist.

1 small	uncut bloomer loaf	1 small
75 g	butter, melted	3 oz
225 g	pork sausagemeat	8 oz
100 g	cooked tongue, chopped	4 oz
50 g	onion, chopped	2 oz
2	eggs	2
150 ml	milk	¼ pint
2	hard-boiled eggs, shelled and halved	2
	salt and pepper	

1. Preheat the oven to moderately hot (200°C, 400°F, Gas Mark 6).
2. Cut horizontally across the loaf with a bread knife, two-thirds of the way up, and remove this 'lid'.
3. Gently ease away the bread from around the edge of the crust, base and lid, and make 100 g/4 oz breadcrumbs from the bread. Brush the inside of the loaf base and lid with some of the melted butter.
4. Place the sausagemeat, tongue, breadcrumbs and onion in a bowl. Mix well with a wooden spoon to blend. Beat the eggs and milk together and stir into the meat mixture.
5. Place one-third of this filling in the bread case and top with the halved hard-boiled eggs. Season with salt and pepper to taste. Top with the remaining meat mixture, packing down well. Cover with the bread lid.
6. Secure the loaf in a parcel-like fashion with string and place on a baking tray. Brush all over with the remaining butter.
7. Cook in the oven for 15 minutes. Remove and cover with foil. Return to the oven and cook for a further 45 minutes. Leave until cold.
8. Remove the string and cut into thick slices to serve. **Serves 8**

Melon, Orange and Ginger Cocktail
(Illustrated on page 54)

This is a light refreshing dessert that is perfect to eat out-of-doors during the hot summer months.

1 teaspoon	ground ginger	1 teaspoon
100 g	granulated sugar	4 oz
4 tablespoons	water	4 tablespoons
1 large	Honeydew melon (or other in season as liked)	1 large
3 large	oranges	3 large
3	kiwi fruit	3

1. Place the ginger, sugar and water in a small saucepan and heat gently until the sugar dissolves. Bring to the boil and cook for 5 minutes to make a syrup. Allow to cool then chill in the refrigerator.
2. Meanwhile, halve the melon and scoop out the seeds. Peel away the skin with a sharp knife and cut the flesh into cubes or 'dig' out balls using a special melon baller. Place in a mixing bowl.
3. Cut a slice from each end of the oranges. Set, cut side down, on a chopping board and carefully slice away the skin, in downward strokes, removing the pith but very little flesh. Then free the segments of orange by slicing between the radiating pith on either side of each fruit segment. Add to the melon in the bowl.
4. Carefully peel the hairy skin from the kiwi fruit using a serrated knife then cut across the flesh into thin slices. Add to the melon and orange.
5. Pour the cold syrup over the fruit and chill for about 1 hour. Serve chilled. **Serves 4–6**

Special Feature
Know Your Melons

There is a melon in season almost every month of the year. To check for ripeness, gently press the stalk end – it should feel soft. The melon should also sound hollow when tapped. In Britain we can choose from:

Galia Melon A round melon with golden, bark-like skin and pale green flesh. It is in season from April to December.

Ogen Melon A round melon with yellow skin and green stripes and a pale green flesh. It is in season from April to December.

Honeydew Melon An oval melon with bright yellow skin and pale gold flesh. It is in season from May to July and October to January.

Watermelon A large melon with dark green skin and bright red flesh with black pips. It is in season from May to mid-July.

Bottom, Bacon Bridies (opposite); *centre left*, Bow Tie Salad (opposite);
top, Melon, Orange and Ginger Cocktail (page 53); *centre right* Raspberry Yogurt Jellies (page 50).

Bacon Bridies
(Illustrated opposite)

Bacon Bridies are scrumptious pastries stuffed fit-to-burst with bacon, onion, carrots and potatoes. They are delicious hot or cold and prove ideal food to take on a picnic.

225 g	shortcrust pastry (see page 16)	8 oz
	Filling	
15 g	butter	$\frac{1}{2}$ oz
225 g	middlecut bacon, rinded and chopped	8 oz
1	onion peeled and chopped	1
100 g	carrots, peeled and chopped	4 oz
100 g	potatoes peeled and chopped	4 oz
1 teaspoon	dried mixed herbs	1 teaspoon
1 tablespoon	chopped parsley	1 tablespoon
	pepper	
	beaten egg to glaze	

1. Preheat the oven to moderately hot (200°C, 400°F, Gas Mark 6).
2. Roll out the pastry on a lightly floured surface until thin. Cut around an upside-down saucer to make six rounds of pastry, re-rolling the pastry as necessary.
3. Place the butter in a saucepan and heat to melt. Add the bacon and onion and fry for 5 minutes.
4. Add the carrots, potatoes, herbs, parsley and pepper to taste. Continue to fry for a further 5 minutes. Allow to cool completely.
5. Divide the bacon mixture into six portions and place each in the centre of a pastry round. Brush the edges with beaten egg using a pastry brush and fold over the pastry to make a turnover or semi-circular pasty. Pinch the edges together to seal and to give an attractive finish. Brush with beaten egg to glaze.
6. Place on a greased baking tray and bake for 10 minutes. Reduce the oven temperature to 190°C, 375°F, Gas Mark 5 and cook for a further 20 minutes. Serve hot or cold. **Makes 6**

Bow Tie Salad
(Illustrated opposite)

This salad travels well for a picnic or packed lunch.

225 g	pasta bow ties	8 oz
225 g	cooked ham, cut into thin strips	8 oz
100 g	mushrooms, wiped and sliced	4 oz
1	red or yellow pepper, cored, seeded and sliced	1
4	spring onions, chopped	4
8	radishes, trimmed and sliced	8
	Dressing	
150 ml	salad oil	$\frac{1}{4}$ pint
3 tablespoons	wine vinegar	3 tablespoons
1 tablespoon	tomato purée	1 tablespoon
1 teaspoon	poppy seeds	1 teaspoon
2 teaspoons	dried mixed herbs	2 teaspoons
	salt and pepper	

1. Place the pasta bow ties in a pan of boiling salted water and cook for about 10 minutes until just tender. Drain through a colander and leave until cold. Place in a mixing bowl.
2. Add the ham, mushrooms, pepper, spring onions and radishes. Mix well to blend.
3. Meanwhile, place all the salad dressing ingredients in a screw-topped jar and shake vigorously until very well mixed.
4. Pour over the pasta salad and stir well until all the ingredients are coated with the dressing. Chill before serving. **Serves 4–6**

Special Feature
Pasta Shapes

Long strands of spaghetti, nests of tagliatelle, twists, rings, wheels and spaceships; no other food comes in such a variety of shapes and sizes as pasta.

Shells, bow ties, rings, waggon wheels, stars, cocks' combs, spirals and alphabets are all self-explanatory shapes. More puzzling are the following:

Penne This is a pasta shape that looks like a pen quill.
Fettucini A folded nest of ribbon fine noodles that unwrap when cooked.
Vermicelli Very thin or fine spaghetti type pasta.
Twistetti Curly twists of pasta cut into short lengths.
Elbow macaroni Quarter moons of hollow pasta shaped rather like a bent elbow.

FOODIE GIFTS TO MAKE

Tiffin Biscuits

Tiffin biscuits are delicious biscuit fingers made with raisins, chocolate, digestive biscuits and cherries. They make delicious lunch box goodies or gifts to give away on special occasions. They will keep in a cool place for up to 1 week.

	Base	
100 g	butter	4 oz
3 tablespoons	golden syrup	3 tablespoons
225 g	digestive biscuits	8 oz
50 g	raisins	2 oz
50 g	glacé cherries, quartered	2 oz
175 g	plain chocolate, chopped	6 oz
	Topping	
75 g	plain chocolate	3 oz
25 g	butter	1 oz
25 g	icing sugar	1 oz
1 tablespoon	milk	1 tablespoon

1. Line an 18-cm/7-inch shallow square tin with foil.
2. Place the butter and golden syrup in a saucepan and heat gently until the butter melts, stirring occasionally.
3. Meanwhile, place the biscuits in a plastic bag and crush with a rolling pin until they form fine crumbs.
4. Add to the butter mixture with the raisins, cherries and chocolate. Mix well to blend.
5. Press the biscuit mixture firmly into the prepared tin and level the surface with the back of a spoon. Leave in a cool place to set.
6. When set, make the icing by placing the chocolate and butter in a bowl set over a saucepan of hot water. Stir until the chocolate and butter melt. Add the icing sugar and beat well until smooth and glossy. Add the milk and beat well.
7. Quickly spread over the biscuit mixture and chill to set.
8. When set cut into about 14 fingers with a knife.
9. Pack in a greaseproof or wax paper-lined box or see-through cellophane bag for giving. Tie with colourful ribbon or lace for a special gift.

Makes 14 fingers

Coffee Honey Crackles

In order to make 450 g/1 lb honey, a bee needs to fly the equivalent of three times around the world collecting nectar and pollen from flowers. This may seem a tall order but not so difficult when you consider that honeybee society revolves around the bee hive which can contain as many as 60,000 bees – a Queen, several hundred male bees or drones and thousands of female workers.

If properly stored, honey never goes bad (recently a jar of honey which was over 5,000 years old was unearthed in Egypt and found to be good). Combined with coffee, rice cereal and butter in the recipe below, it makes 49 delicious crackles that will keep for up to 1 week.

2 tablespoons	clear honey	2 tablespoons
75 g	butter	3 oz
2 teaspoons	instant coffee powder	2 teaspoons
1 tablespoon	hot water	1 tablespoon
175 g	icing sugar	6 oz
100 g	rice cereal (Rice Krispies, for example)	4 oz
150 g	plain chocolate	5 oz

1. Line an 18-cm/7-inch square cake tin with greaseproof paper.
2. Place the honey and butter in a saucepan and heat gently until the butter melts, stirring occasionally.
3. Meanwhile, dissolve the coffee powder in the hot water in a small bowl.
4. Remove the saucepan from the heat and stir in the coffee mixture, icing sugar and rice cereal, mixing well so that all the cereal is coated and sticks together.
5. Press the mixture into the tin and level the surface. Leave in a cool place to set.
6. When set, make the topping by placing the chocolate in a bowl set over a saucepan of hot water. Stir until the chocolate melts. Spread over the honey crackle mixture and leave to set.
7. When set, cut into 2.5-cm/1-inch squares with a knife.
8. Pack into a greaseproof or wax paper-lined box or see-through cellophane bag for giving. Tie with colourful ribbon or lace for a special gift.

Makes 49 pieces

Salted Nuts
(Illustrated on page 59)

Everyone seems to love salted nuts so they can make a very welcome gift at Christmas or birthday time. For a special thought check out your friend or relative's favourite nut flavour – herb, garlic, curry, celery or plain salt.

25 g	butter	1 oz
225 g	flaked almonds	8 oz
	salt to sprinkle	

1. Place the butter in a frying pan and heat gently to melt.
2. Add the flaked almonds and fry over a gentle heat until golden, stirring constantly.
3. Remove from the heat and drain on a double thickness sheet of absorbent kitchen paper.
4. Sprinkle with salt to taste while still hot. Leave until cold.
5. Pack into clean, dry screw-topped jars, sealing well. Store in a cool place for up to 2 weeks.

Makes 225 g/8 oz (enough for 1–2 small jars)

Variations

Herby Salted Nuts Prepare as above but cook with 1–2 teaspoons dried mixed herbs and the butter.
Garlicky Salted Nuts Prepare as above but sprinkle with garlic salt after cooking.
Curried Salted Nuts Prepare as above but sprinkle with a little curry powder and salt after cooking.
Celery Salted Nuts Prepare as above but sprinkle with celery salt after cooking.

Hazelnut and Ginger Clusters
(Illustrated on page 59)

In the recipe below it is necessary to use skinned nuts. The easiest way to do this is to place the nuts on a grill tray and to cook, under a preheated hot grill, until the skins just turn dark brown and crisp, shaking the nuts from time to time to crisp evenly on all sides. Remove and leave until cold. Rub the nuts between the palms of your hands or in a clean tea towel to remove the skins – they will slip easily away.

50 g	hazelnuts, skinned	2 oz
75 g	plain chocolate	3 oz
50 g	crystallised ginger	2 oz

1. Place the skinned hazelnuts on a board and coarsely chop into small pieces with a knife.
2. Place the chocolate in a bowl set over a saucepan of hot water. Stir until the chocolate melts.
3. Finely chop the crystallised ginger into small pieces. Add the hazelnuts and half the ginger to the chocolate and mix well to blend.
4. Spoon the chocolate mixture equally into 12 paper sweet cases, using a teaspoon.
5. Sprinkle with the remaining ginger and leave to set.
6. To pack as a gift, place the clusters in a box with a see-through lid and tie with a colourful ribbon.

Makes 12

Blackberry Fool

This is a delicious, simple-to-make dessert, ideal when blackberries are cheap and plentiful for the picking.

450 g	blackberries	1 lb
75 g	light brown sugar	3 oz
	juice of 1 small lemon	
300 ml	double cream	$\frac{1}{2}$ pint
	blackberries to decorate	

1. Hull the blackberries and wash in a colander. Drain thoroughly.
2. Place in a saucepan with the sugar, lemon juice and 1 tablespoon water. Cook over a very gentle heat until soft. This will take about 10–12 minutes, stirring occasionally.
3. Purée in a blender or pass through a nylon sieve into a bowl. Cover and chill in the refrigerator for 1 hour.
4. Whip the cream until stiff then slowly add the blackberry purée until well blended.
5. Spoon into individual glass serving dishes and chill for 30 minutes. Frost the rims of the glasses with sugar if liked before carefully adding the fool (see below).
6. Serve decorated with a few whole blackberries.

Serves 4

Special Feature
Frosting the Rims of Glasses

Special desserts and drinks can look all the more special or festive if you colourfully frost the rim of the glass.

Simply dip the rim of the glass in a little lightly beaten egg white, or paint the egg white around with a small brush, then dip in plain or tinted caster sugar. Refrigerate until the rim looks frosty and dry.

Lemon Curd
(Illustrated opposite)

Lemon juice is a very important ingredient in this recipe where the juice of 3 medium lemons is needed. If you are not sure whether your lemons are the right size then remember that 1 medium lemon yields 3 tablespoons of juice when squeezed.

3	medium lemons	3
100 g	butter	4 oz
225 g	granulated sugar	8 oz
3	eggs, beaten	3
1	egg yolk, beaten	1

1. Finely grate the rind and squeeze the juice from the lemons.
2. Place the butter in a bowl set over a saucepan of gently simmering water and stir to melt.
3. Add the sugar, eggs, egg yolk, lemon rind and juice. Mix very well to blend.
4. Continue to cook gently *without boiling* until the mixture will coat the back of a wooden spoon, stirring constantly and checking that the mixture does not overheat or it could curdle and separate. This may take up to 20 minutes.
5. Pour into clean, dry, warmed jars. Press a well-fitting waxed lid on the surface of each jar of lemon curd and wipe the rim carefully with a hot, damp cloth. Leave to cool.
6. When cold cover the jars with cellophane or cling film lids and secure with rubber bands.
7. To decorate as a gift you may like to cover the tops with discs of colourful material and secure with ribbon. Make labels to stick on the jars saying who they are for, when made and any other special greeting. Store in a very cool place for up to 2 weeks. **Makes about 675 g/1½ lb**

Chocolate Truffle Logs
(Illustrated opposite)

These delicious log-shaped truffles can be made in the traditional round ball shape if preferred. Roll in long-thread coconut, chopped nuts or powdered chocolate, or a mixture of all three, for a different effect.

75 g	plain chocolate	3 oz
1 teaspoon	single cream	1 teaspoon
1	egg yolk	1
7 g	butter	¼ oz
1 teaspoon	milk	1 teaspoon
40 g	chocolate vermicelli	1½ oz

1. Place the chocolate in a bowl set over a saucepan of hot water. Stir until the chocolate melts.
2. Remove from the heat and add the cream, egg yolk, butter and milk. Beat very well to blend. Continue beating until cool and thick. This will take about 5–10 minutes. Chill in the refrigerator until lightly set.
3. Using a teaspoon, divide the mixture into about 15 portions and shape each, in the palm of your hands, to a small log. Do not over-handle or the mixture will melt.
4. Place the chocolate vermicelli on a plate and roll the truffle logs in the vermicelli to coat.
5. Place in small paper sweet cases to serve. Store in a cool place for up to 2 weeks. This mixture can also be frozen if liked. **Makes 15**

Petticoat Tails
(Illustrated opposite)

Petticoat tails are pieces of thin crisp shortbread. Their unusual name is thought to have originated from their likeness in shape to the bell-hoop petticoats worn by court ladies in times gone by.

300 g	plain flour	11 oz
50 g	rice flour	2 oz
150 g	butter	5 oz
4 tablespoons	milk	4 tablespoons
50 g	caster sugar	2 oz

1. Preheat the oven to moderate (180°C, 350°F, Gas Mark 4).
2. Sift the plain flour and rice flour into a bowl. Make a well in the middle.
3. Place the butter and milk in a saucepan and heat gently until the butter melts, stirring occasionally.
4. Pour on to the flour and add the sugar. When cool, mix with your fingers to form a light dough. Knead very lightly to keep the shortbread flaky.
5. Roll out on a lightly floured surface to a round about 5 mm/¼ inch thick.
6. Cover with an upside-down dinner plate and trim around the edge with a sharp knife. Remove the dinner plate. Place an upside down wine glass in the centre and cut around this to make a small round. Keeping the centre unmarked, cut the outer ring into eight segments or petticoat tails.
7. Place all the shortbread pieces on a greased baking tray and bake for 20 minutes until pale golden and crisp. Lift from the tray with a spatula and leave to cool on a wire rack.
8. When cool re-assemble the biscuit pattern on a large plate to serve. Alternatively, pack in a large round greaseproof paper-lined box for giving. **Makes 9 pieces**

Bottom left, Salted nuts (page 57); *centre left*, Lemon Curd (opposite); *top left*, Petticoat Tails (opposite); *top right*, Hazelnut and Ginger usters (page 57); *centre*, Orange Pomander (page 60); *centre right*, Tiffin Biscuits (page 56); *bottom right*, Chocolate Truffle Logs (opposite).

Orange Pomander
(Illustrated on page 59)

A pomander is a sweet-smelling ball of exotic spices, usually hung in the wardrobe, linen cupboard or cloakroom for its fragrance and ability to discourage cloth-eating moths.

They were very popular in Elizabethan times in England when worn by the gentry to sweeten the air around themselves and to prevent infection. They make beautiful gifts and are well worth the time taken to prepare carefully. Each pomander will take about 1 hour to stud before drying.

To ring the changes, why not try using a small grapefruit, lemon or lime instead of the orange in the recipe below.

\multicolumn{3}{c}{**For each pomander**}		
1	firm unblemished orange	1
2 small jars	whole cloves	2 small jars
15 g	powdered orris root	½ oz
15 g	ground cinnamon	½ oz
1 metre	colourful ribbon	1 yard

1. Carefully stud the orange with the cloves, making sure that they are studded very carefully together and that no fruit skin shows through.
2. Mix the orris root and cinnamon together on a plate.
3. Roll the studded orange in the mixture to thoroughly coat.
4. Leave in a warm place like an airing cupboard for 3–4 days to dry out.
5. To decorate with a hanging ribbon, tie the ribbon in two vertical circles around the pomander, securing very firmly at the top with the loose ends. Tie the loose ribbon ends together to form a loop and finish with a small bow. **Makes 1**

Mouth-watering Butterscotch

Butterscotch has nothing to do with Scotch whisky but came about simply because the sugar and butter in this recipe were 'scotched' or scorched during cooking!

A candy or sweet thermometer is useful in preparing the recipe but not essential (see 'Sugar Thermometers and Stages of Sugar Boiling' right).

450 g	granulated sugar	1 lb
300 ml	milk	½ pint
175 g	butter	6 oz
\multicolumn{3}{c}{pinch of cream of tartar}		

1. Lightly butter an 18-cm/7-inch square tin.
2. Place the sugar and milk in a large heavy-based saucepan. Heat gently to dissolve the sugar.
3. Add the butter in small pieces and stir to melt. Clip a candy or sugar thermometer, if used, to the side of the pan so that the mercury in the base is resting in the butterscotch mixture.
4. Stir in the cream of tartar and bring to the boil. Continue to boil until the temperature on the thermometer reaches 118°C/245°F, or until a little of the mixture dropped into a cup of cold water forms a firm ball.
5. Quickly pour into the prepared tin. Mark into squares when almost set with a buttered knife.
6. Break up when cold and set. Wrap in waxed paper and tie with a ribbon as a gift. Alternatively, pack in small glass-stoppered jars and seal well with sellotape. Decorate with ribbon if liked. **Makes about 40 pieces**

Special Feature

Sugar Thermometers and Stages of Sugar Boiling

If you intend to make sweets on a regular basis, it would prove worthwhile to buy a special candy or sugar thermometer. This will tell you by temperature when a mixture will set hard and soft and the degrees between.

Alternatively, you can simply drop a little of the mixture into a cup of cold water and judge for yourself whether the mixture is at the right temperature and stage of cooking.

The following temperatures are equivalent to the various stages required in sweet-making:

Quick Temperature Guide

Temperature	Stage
102–104°C / 215–220°F	Smooth, syrupy or thread stage. The syrup will form a firm thread when the correct temperature has been reached.
113–118°C / 235–245°F	Soft ball stage. The mixture flattens easily when pressed between the fingers after dropping in water. Stage used in making fudge.
118–130°C / 245–265°F	Firm or hard ball stage. The mixture will form a hard but pliable ball after dropping in water. Stage used in making caramels.
132–143°C / 270–290°F	Soft crack stage. The mixture separates into soft but brittle threads when dropped into water. Stage used for making toffees.
149–154°C / 300–310°F	Hard crack stage. The mixture forms hard brittle threads when dropped into water. Stage used for making hard toffees.
154°C / 310°F	Caramel stage. The syrup turns a light golden colour.

INDEX

Numbers in italics refer to captions.

American hamburgers 50, *51*
apple
   and leek soup *51*, 52
   types of 52
aubergines, dégorging 40

bacon
   bridies *54*, 55
   leek, bacon and tomato risotto 28
   nesting eggs *22*, 23
   spaghetti and bacon omelette *22*, 23
baked eggs 13
baking "blind" 32
banana and walnut loaf 41, *43*
barbecues, impromptu 50
bean
   mung beans 33
   pizza *27*, 28
   sprouting beans 33
beansprouts 33
beef
   and orange risotto 32
   roasting 14
biscuit squares, tiffin 56, *59*
blackberry fool 57
"blind" baking 32
boiled eggs 12
bow tie salad *54*, 55
bread, white 17
breakfast fruit salad 18, *19*
brownies, chocolate 42, *43*
butters, flavoured 29
butterscotch, mouth-watering 60

cake
   hot air balloon *6*, 49
   Victoria sandwich *15*, 17
cake tins, lining *15*, 41
Cheddar sails *6*, 44
cheese
   Cheddar sails *6*, 44
   cheesy oatburgers 26, *27*
   cheesy party nibbles 46, *47*
   coconut lemon cheese flan 42, *43*
   English 26
   super macaroni 24
cheesecake, orange *38*, 39
cheesy
   oatburgers 26, *27*
   party nibbles 46, *47*
chicken and ham stir-fried rice 33
chocolate
   brownies 42, *43*
   honey and chocolate yule log 45
   moon rocket 45
   truffle logs 58, *59*
chutney, green tomato *51*, 52
citrus
   fruit garnishes 42
   start, grilled 20
coconut lemon cheese flan 42, *43*
clapping eggs *4*, 37
cocktail, melon, orange and ginger 53, *54*
coffee
   honey crackles 56
   making 12
coloured Easter eggs *47*, 48
cream, soured 18
creaming ingredients 10
creams, Jamaican *38*, 41
creamy porridge 21
crunchy muesli 18, *19*
curd, lemon 58, *59*
custard sauce 16

Easter eggs, coloured *47*, 48

eggs
   bacon nesting *22*, 23
   baked 13
   boiled 12
   checking for freshness 39
   clapping *4*, 37
   coloured Easter eggs *47*, 48
   fried 12
   hard-boiled 24
   omelettes 13, *22*, 23, 29
   poached 12–13
   scrambled 13
   separating 30
   supeme scrambled 20

fishy jacket potatoes 25, *27*
flan
   coconut lemon cheese 42, *43*
   tuna fish 32
folding ingredients 10
fool, blackberry 57
fried eggs 12
frosting glass rims 57
fruit
   breakfast fruit salad 18, *19*
   citrus fruit garnishes 42
   see also individual type of fruit

game, roasting 14
garnishes, citrus fruit 42
ginger
   hazelnut and ginger clusters 57, *59*
   marrow, rhubarb and ginger jam 21
   melon, orange and ginger cocktail 53, *54*
glass rims, frosting 57
grape salad, pear and green 34, *35*
gravy 14
green tomato chutney *51*, 52
grilled citrus start 20

ham
   chicken and ham stir-fried rice 33
   club sandwich 29
hamburgers, American 50, *51*
hard-boiled eggs 24
hazelnut and ginger clusters 57, *59*
herbs, garden 26
herby mushroom and pâté toasted sandwiches 33
honey
   and chocolate yule log 45
   coffee honey crackles 56
   honeyed prunes 20
hot air balloon cake *6*, 49
hot dogs *31*, 32

ice cream, tasty lemon *38*, 39
icing bag, paper 49

jacket potatoes, fishy 25, *27*
jam
   marrow, rhubarb and ginger 21
   setting point 21
Jamaican creams *38*, 41
jellies, raspberry yoghurt 50, *54*

kedgeree *22*, 23
kipper toasts 21
kitchen equipment 9–10, *11*
kneading ingredients 10

lamb, roasting 14
leek
   apple and leek soup *51*, 52
   bacon and tomato risotto 28

lemon
   coconut lemon cheese flan 42, *43*
   curd 58, *59*
   tasty lemon ice cream *38*, 39
loaf, banana and walnut 41, *43*

macaroni cheese, super 24
marrow, rhubarb and ginger jam 21
measuring ingredients 10
Mediterranean omelette 29
melon
   orange and ginger cocktail 53, *54*
   types of 53
Mexican spaghetti supper 24
mince, savoury, with crumble thatch *4*, 37
Mothering Sunday nest 46, *47*
moussaka 34, *35*
mouth-watering butterscotch 60
muesli
   crunchy 18, *19*
   pear muesli with yoghurt *19*, 20
mung beans 33
mushroom, herby, and pâté toasted sandwiches 33

nibbles, cheesy party *47*, 48
nuts
   hazelnut and ginger clusters 57
   salted 57, *59*

oatburgers, cheesy 26
omelette pan, seasoning 29
omelettes 13
   Mediterranean 29
   spaghetti and bacon *22*, 23
one pan sausage supper *4*, 40
orange
   beef and orange risotto 32
   cheesecake *38*, 39
   melon, orange and ginger cocktail 53, *54*
   pomander 60
   sunrise 18, *19*
oven temperatures 8

pancakes, savoury spicy 25
pasta 13, 24, 36, 55
pastry, shortcrust 16
pâté toasted sandwiches, herby mushroom and 33
pear
   Comice 34
   Conference 34
   and green grape salad 34, *35*
   muesli with yoghurt *19*, 20
petticoat tails 58, *59*
picnic sandwich box 53
pizza
   bean *27*, 28
   speedy *6*, 40
poached eggs 12–13
pomander, orange *59*, 60
pork
   roasting 14
   sweet 'n' sour *35*, 36
porridge, creamy 21
potatoes, fishy jacket 25, *27*
poultry, roasting 14
prunes, honeyed 20
puréed ingredients 10

raspberry yoghurt jellies 50, *54*
rhubarb and ginger jam, marrow 21
rice
   chicken and ham stir-fried 33
   long-grain 13
rice pudding 16

risotto
   beef and orange 32
   leek, bacon and tomato 28
roasting 14
rubbing in ingredients 10

safety in kitchen 8
salad
   bow tie *54*, 55
   breakfast fruit salad 18, *19*
   pear and green grape 34, *35*
salted nuts 57, *59*
sandwich
   ham club 29
   herby mushroom and pâté toasted sandwiches 33
   picnic sandwich box 53
   spinning catherine wheel sandwich board 44
sauces
   custard 16
   white coating 13
sausage
   one pan sausage supper *4*, 40
   wrappers *47*, 48
sausagemeat volcano, spaghetti and 36
savoury
   mince with crumble thatch *4*, 37
   spicy pancakes 25
scones *15*, 17
scrambled eggs 13
   supreme 20
separating eggs 30
souffléed Welsh rarebit 30, *31*
soup, apple and leek *51*, 52
soured cream 18
spaghetti
   and bacon omelette *22*, 23
   Mexican spaghetti supper 24
   and sausagemeat volcano 36
special custard sauce 16
speedy pizza *6*, 40
spices 52
spicy pancakes, savoury 25
spinning catherine wheel sandwich board 44
sponge igloo 48
stir-fried rice, chicken and ham 33
sugar boiling 60
super macaroni cheese 24
supreme scrambled eggs 20
sweet 'n' sour pork *35*, 36

tasty lemon ice cream *38*, 39
tea, making 12
tiffin biscuits 56, *59*
tomatoes
   green tomato chutney *51*, 52
   leek, bacon and tomato risotto 28
   peeling 28
tuna fish flan 32

Union Jack snack 30, *31*

veal, roasting 14
vegetable cooking, basic 14
Victoria sandwich *15*, 17

walnut loaf, banana and 41, *43*
Welsh rarebit, souffléed 30, *31*
whipping ingredients 10
whisking ingredients 10
white coating sauce 13

yoghurt
   pear muesli with *19*, 20
   raspberry yoghurt jellies 50, *54*
Yorkshire pudding 16
yule log, honey and chocolate 45